FRANK O'CONNOR (pseudonym of Michael O'Donovan) was born in Cork in 1903. His childhood and adolescence in Cork, much of it spent in poverty, is reflected in his first volume of autobiography *An Only Child* (1961), and in the novels *The Saint and Mary Kate* (1932) and *Dutch Interior* (1940), all recently reprinted by Blackstaff Press. He fought on the republican side in the Irish Civil War (1922–3) and was imprisoned in Gormanstown during this time. The political turmoil of that period is described in his first volume of short stories, *Guests of the Nation* (1931), and his biography of Michael Collins, *The Big Fellow* (1937). *My Father's Son* (1968), his second volume of autobiography, begins with his release from prison. Active in the Irish literary revival of the 1930s and 1940s, he was a director of the Abbey Theatre and poetry editor of *The Bell*. Frustrated by official censorship of his work, he left Ireland in 1950 to accept invitations to teach in the United States, where his short stories won great critical acclaim. At the time of his death in 1966, O'Connor's reputation was assured and his work continues to have an enduring influence on modern literature and Irish life.

MY
FATHER'S SON

FRANK O'CONNOR

THE
BLACKSTAFF
PRESS

BELFAST

First published in hardback in 1968
by Macmillan and Company Limited and in paperback in 1971
by Pan Books Limited

This Blackstaff Press edition is a photolithographic facsimile of the
first edition printed by Robert Maclehose and Company Limited, Glasgow

This paperback edition published in 1994 by
The Blackstaff Press Limited
3 Galway Park, Dundonald, Belfast BT16 0AN, Northern Ireland
with the assistance of
The Arts Council of Northern Ireland

Printed by The Guernsey Press Company Limited

A catalogue record for this book is available from the British Library

ISBN 0-85640-522-1

CONTENTS

When Frank O'Connor died on 10 March 1966, he had not completed this second volume of his autobiography, *My Father's Son*. Much of it existed in early drafts, some of it in separate pieces. We are indebted to Dr Maurice Sheehy of University College, Dublin for comparing the different drafts and producing the present text.

PART ONE

RISING IN THE WORLD

I

AT the age of twenty I was released from an internment camp without money or job. The Civil War had just ended, and since I had taken the loser's side I found that ex-gaolbirds like myself did not get whatever positions were available under the new government. But all teachers were now required to learn the Irish language, so for a few months I taught Irish to the teachers at the local Protestant school in Cork – St Luke's. This brought in only a few shillings a week, but I now knew how to teach and I liked the work.

I also liked Kennelly, the headmaster, an irascible little Kerryman who wore pince-nez. I suspect he was a fearful bully and disciplinarian because he always snapped at everyone who came near him, including his pretty daughter, and snapped loudest of all at the school manager, Canon Flewett.

'All clergymen are the same, Mr O'Donovan,' Kennelly would say as he saw me part of the way home. 'Catholic, Church of Ireland or Presbyterian, you can never trust any of them.'

It was part of his innocent vanity that I could never teach him Irish because he remembered it all perfectly from his childhood in Kerry. But he was a man with a real flavour, and I enjoyed watching him when someone got him mad, keeping what he thought was a perfectly expressionless face, though his little nose took on an autonomous life and expressed a whole range of emotions that no pince-nez could stand up to. In spite of his snappiness he was extraordinarily gentle with me; he even brought me home once or twice to supper with his wife and daughter, but I was so embarrassed that I do not even remember what nonsense I talked; and when he saw me home it was to advise me in a fatherly way to have nothing more to do with politics.

'With you it's not a question of politics,' he said, referring delicately to the fact that I was still wearing Father's old trousers. 'It's a question of how much a man can take, and you've taken enough. You can't afford to take any more.'

One of the pleasantest revelations that life has offered was that on his retirement that stout anti-clerical rushed himself into Holy Orders and worked gallantly as a missioner in the East End of London through the blitz. All Irish anti-clericals are spoiled priests, and you must never trust any of them.

Late in 1923 my old teacher Daniel Corkery told me that Lennox Robinson, the dramatist, who was now Secretary of the Irish Carnegie United Kingdom Trust, was organizing rural libraries and looking for young men and women to train as librarians. The moment he said it I knew that this was the very job for me and that I was the very type of person Robinson was looking for. It was not so much that I wanted to be a librarian, or even knew what being a librarian meant; it was just that never in my life had I had enough books to read and this was my opportunity.

I met Robinson in the restaurant of the Cork railway station at Glanmire, where he was waiting for a train to Dublin and drinking double brandies. He always looked like someone's caricature of him, long and mournful and disjointed, as though at some time he had suffered on the rack, and he had a high-pitched, disjointed voice that sounded like someone's reading of an old maid's letter from Regency times, with every third word isolated and emphasized.

The only sort of job he could offer me sounded hopeless. I should have to spend a year or two studying librarianship somewhere in the north of Ireland, and the salary would be thirty shillings a week, though at the end of my training I should qualify for a librarian's post at two hundred and fifty pounds a year. The latter figure, of course, was fantastic; I couldn't imagine what anyone would do with five pounds a week, but even in the twenties I knew that nobody could live away from home on thirty shillings a week. I could manage it at home, but not in lodgings.

I have met some tough bargainers in my life, but none quite so ruthless as Robinson. He merely looked ineffectual and sad, and God did not choose to reveal to me that within a few years *he* would be begging for a job from me and I would not have the sense to look ineffectual and sad, so I went home in great distress to my mother.

She, poor woman, did not have much sense either, but she saw clearly that a job in a library was about the only job I was qualified for, and she timidly offered to add half a crown, or even – if she was lucky – five shillings to the salary till something better turned up. I hated to accept her offer because I knew how she would have to earn it.

But, shortly after, she got a loan to buy me a decent little cardboard suitcase and packed it with my spare shirt and underpants and a few pairs of stockings she had knitted herself. I have a strong recollection that she packed a holy picture as well, for fear I might not find one in an out-of-the-way place like Sligo, and I set out for Dublin on my way to the west, like Cú Chulainn setting out for Armagh at the age of seven, though I was fourteen years older and had nothing of the heroic spirit.

2

I FOUND lodgings near Sligo Cathedral at twenty-seven and sixpence a week and had a whole half-crown for laundry, cigarettes and drink. Mother had worked it out that it would be cheaper to post my laundry home than to get it done locally, and every week I posted home my shirt, my underpants, a pair of stockings and some handkerchiefs.

My room was in the house of an ex-officer in the Free State Army who had been a private soldier in Churchill's campaign against Russia and taught me my first words of Russian. When he was on the drink he was very like Father, and I slept with his rifle under my mattress because his wife was afraid he might use it. One night when he took it out and loaded it, she begged me to stay up and watch with him. It seemed that somebody had been sleeping at the bottom of his garden. Early next morning we stole out of the house and crept down the garden in approved army style to surround and overwhelm the trespasser. She turned out to be a poor country girl from near Collooney who had been thrown out by her parents and had nowhere in the world to go, so my landlord let her off with a caution.

There were other troubles as well. Across the road lived a loyal Protestant, and occasionally in the evening the passions would rise in him at the thought of all the dirty disloyal Catholics about him, and then he would throw open the window and play 'God save the King' on the gramophone. At the first notes of the insulting melody my landlord, an equally staunch supporter of the other side, would drop whatever he was doing and race for my room with a portable gramophone, rest it in the window-sill and play 'The Soldier's Song'. His wife, a decent Cork woman, said that the Sligo people had 'no nature', but I wouldn't have gone as far as that. They struck me as very patriotic.

Robert Wilson, the librarian, was a small nervous man with an irregular face, flushed with whiskey, thick sensuous lips and delightful brown rogue's eyes set a little to the side of his head. By the time I got there Lennox Robinson was on the point of being compelled to resign from his position as Secretary. He had written what had been denounced as a 'blasphemous' story in a little paper called *To-Morrow*, and what Lady Gregory tartly called 'a storm in a chalice' followed. The story concerned a simple country girl who believed she had been visited in the same way as Christ's mother, and, as if to ram the point home, Yeats contributed his sonnet on Leda. When we heard of Robinson's resignation, Wilson buried his head in his hands and moaned, 'O Ireland, how thou stonest thy prophets!', which struck me as excessive.

Wilson was neat and dexterous, and though after a week or two of my clumsiness he gave me up as a bad job and began to introduce me as his 'untrainable assistant' he was extraordinarily kind, drove me to every spot Yeats had written about, and stopped the car while he chanted poems with tears in those gentle, beseeching rogue's eyes; took me home to dinner in his flat and played me Vaughan Williams, and lamented the ugliness of Irish Catholicism (to which he was a convert) and the beastliness of the cathedral music. I liked him and I liked his poems, but I wished he wouldn't bring me home, because at the age of twenty I had never dined out anywhere, and his English society wife could make me mix the cutlery and gag over my dinner like no hostess I ever met after. Years later, it was of her I was thinking when I made a young policeman say of his sergeant's wife that God Almighty had put her in the world with the one main object of persecuting him.

Long after, Wilson and I met when she was dead and he had left the library to return to schoolmastering. Over a drink he told me shyly that he had changed his name to 'Robin', and then produced photographs of the beautiful schoolboy with whom he had just spent a continental holiday. I understood then, too late, the brave face he had been putting on things in those Sligo years and the thick crust of innocence and ignorance that had made it impossible for me to return his kindness.

I wasn't really 'untrainable', as he jokingly complained, but I was not very happy either. Partly I missed Cork, but partly there was a certain air of futility about the work of the library that reminded me a little of the railway.* We had village and small-town branches throughout the country, and every three months we sent them each a box or two of books by rail. We had a printed catalogue of the 'Three Thousand Best Books', and the local secretary made his choice from this, though, as we had only one copy of each book, he rarely got what he asked for. The catalogue of the 'Three Thousand Best Books' had been compiled by an unbookish Belfastman, who was rarely sober, and, like the 'Hundred Best After-Dinner Stories', his choice plunged whole provinces in gloom.

The Belfastman's notion of rural libraries was based on city libraries of the Victorian era, and these in their turn had been based on university libraries. Hence the importance of having only one copy of a book instead of the twenty or thirty copies that were really needed – this would decrease one's 'basic stock'. A library with forty thousand titles was more useful to an imaginary research student, and nobody explained to us that we were not dealing with research students.

All the same, I wasn't entirely unhappy. For the first time in my life I had books at my disposal. Whenever a box was returned from some country centre I fell on it, hoping for treasure – a book of poems or a Russian novel I had not read. I took away the library's *Collected Poems* of Yeats and practically learned it by heart. The local assistant, Bob Lambert, who was almost as hard-up as I was, came on long lonesome walks with me, out to Strandhill or Rosses Point, and we carefully spaced the poems and the cigarettes. Long as the walks were, I do not remember that either of us ever had enough to pay for two bottles of beer. And besides, after I had been in Sligo only for a month or two, the Carnegie Trust summoned Wilson and myself to a conference in

* See *An Only Child*, ch. 14.

London, with all expenses paid, and I dreamed of it for weeks. It was to be my first trip out of Ireland.

And a terrible trip it was. We took ship in Belfast; I was seasick the whole time and thought I was going to drown, so I comforted myself by reciting 'Lycidas' the whole night through. When Wilson came into my cabin next morning I smiled bravely at him and said, 'For Lycidas, your sorrow, is not dead.'

Encouraged, no doubt, by this, he insisted on taking me to Mattins in Liverpool Cathedral, having first explained to me in his kindly way that the Irish bishops' ban on attending Protestant services did not apply in England – as though that worried me. Poor Wilson! In his genuine desire to make an educated man of me he was always going out of his own way to put things in mine – Yeats, Vaughan Williams, English villages and now Mattins.

On the boat we had been joined by MacIntyre, the Donegal librarian, an untidy, harassed little man in glasses, who had been a village postman. Wilson had told me about MacIntyre's visit to Sligo, when he had hung over the bridge, looking at the foaming waters beneath and said solemnly, ' "I would that we were, my beloved, white swans on the foam of the sea!" – God, there's enough watter here to wash all the watter-closets in Sligo.'

Mac, who was a native Irish speaker, did not like the idea of travelling alone in a foreign country, so he attached himself to us, more particularly to me because I spoke Irish almost as well as he did, though he would not have admitted this. Neither, of course, did he like the idea of attending a heretical service, and the moment a prayer began he ran quivering to the west door and stood there till the organ began again.

'Och, such a nice cathedral!' he clucked at me. 'Such a pity it isn't our own!'

At the other side Wilson turned beseeching brown eyes on me whenever he particularly wanted me to admire the service; and at last he could stand it no longer and joined in himself. As a Catholic he should not have done this, but as a parson's son he simply could not resist. Between the two guilty creatures I felt like

Goethe's description of himself – *Propheten rechts, Propheten links, das Weltkind in der Mitte*. I was inconceivably worldly.

MacIntyre attached himself to me all the time in London and insisted not only on staying in the same hotel, but on sleeping in the same bedroom. He also refused to speak anything but Irish, which was a sore trial to me as I spoke Munster Irish, which has been infected by the accentuation of Norman-French, and he spoke Ulster Irish, which has been affected by Scottish Gaelic. It was only a question of the tonic accent, of whether you said 'P'cheen' or 'Potin', but oh, dear God, the trial that tonic accent could become when MacIntyre became glued with fright in the middle of Piccadilly Circus and would neither come on nor go back.

He had tried to buy for Donegal County Library a book which he thought was very devotional – it was Joyce's *Portrait of the Artist as a Young Man* – and had actually bought an anthology of contemporary French poetry. One night at bedtime he begged me to read to him from this. From listening to Wilson's French I knew how deplorable my own French accent was, but he was so much in earnest that I read him Jammes' 'Prayer to Go to Heaven With the Donkeys'. It put MacIntyre into a state of ecstasy.

'Och, man dear,' he said at last, 'isn't it a terrible pity you can't speak Irish as well as you speak French!'

Ulstermen are the nicest people in the world except in the matter of religion and dialect.

I am sure he saw little of London because my London was not one that anyone else would recognize. We must have seen Westminster Bridge because it would have been an excuse for my reciting 'Earth has not anything to show more fair' to him, but I doubt if we ever saw Westminster Abbey. On the other hand I rapidly made myself an authority on London bookshops, and knew the shortest possible route from anywhere through Charing Cross Road to Mudie's or the Times Book Club, and I moved in a lover's trance through the wet twilight, clutching under my arm some treasure I had gone without lunch to buy.

And under the lust for books and pictures was another lust – the provincial's for the strange book or print or packet of cigarettes or bottle of wine that may bring back into the gloom of some provincial town a flash of glory from the world outside. He imagines he can open the book, and there will be Charing Cross Road, or light a Gauloise and back will come the Boulevard St-Michel, but the glory fades; the book becomes like any other book, the print like those he bought in Patrick Street; the cigarettes and wine lose their flavour, which was never theirs to begin with.

Nevertheless the trip had its compensations. A few weeks later I returned to Cork for the Christmas holidays and a little crowd gathered in Corkery's front room on a Sunday night. He was discussing modern architecture and sculpture and spoke severely of Liverpool Cathedral. I protested, and said it wasn't as bad as all that, and Corkery turned on me with unusual severity. I think by this time he felt I was getting notions. 'What do you know about it?' he asked. 'The photographs are there. The detail is *very* bad.' I was embarrassed, because though I might high-hat the neighbours, it would never have occurred to me to be anything but deferential to him, so I said feebly, 'Oh, nothing, but I was there at Mattins a few weeks ago, and I thought it very impressive.' It was only in the silence that followed that I realized that, quite without intending to do so, I had left my old master with nothing at all to say.

3

AFTER six months in Sligo I was sent as assistant to Wicklow, where a new library was to be opened. With me went a second assistant called Brennan, an ex-seminarist who later in life abandoned his literary career and went back to the priesthood.

I lodged in a little huxter shop kept by a widow named Soames on the main street. The house itself seemed to be slipping gently away down from the street into the river. When you opened the unlocked half of the glass front door, there were steps down into the shop, which never seemed to have anything but a few packets on its quite substantial shelving. Then a bell rang and Mrs Soames, with an old coat thrown round her shoulders, came grousing and moaning up another step from the kitchen, which was on the right. She had a long, bloodless white face and the air of an old witch. Behind the shop was the sitting-room, also down a step, but this did little to reduce the house's urge to subside, for the floor sloped alarmingly towards the little window, and the midday soup usually overflowed onto the table-cloth.

I had the room to myself, except for one night in the week when a travelling teacher came. He was small and neat and fussy, with a rosy face and bright blue eyes. He had a poor opinion of Ireland, and when this made him too depressed, he took a couple of drinks. They only made the depression worse, and he kicked his school-books round the room and broke into a nasal wail.

'I'm a child of the sun, and what am I doing with my life? Teaching Eskimos up at the bloody North Pole. This is an awful country!'

Then he took up a Greek play and started to read it to me. When I said I didn't understand it, he became impatient.

'But can't you feel it, man? Can't you feel the Greek sunlight?'

Bill Soames, the only son, was about thirty-five. He was an agricultural labourer, and every morning, wet and fine, cycled miles out into the country to earn his miserable wages. For close on fifteen years he had been keeping company with a servant girl, and each week on her free night they went for a walk or to the cinema. In due course – maybe, if God was good, within the next ten years – his mother would die and leave him the little shop and Bridie could make a few shillings selling cigarettes and keeping a lodger as his mother did.

It was a house of character, and very pleasant on those winter evenings when the rain lashed the window and you heard the roar of shingle from beyond the Murrough, the curious bar of land that divided river from sea.

Geoffrey Phibbs, my boss, was tall and thin and dark, with a long lock of black hair that fell over one eye, a stiff, abrupt manner, a curt high-pitched voice and a rather insolent air. There was something about him that was vaguely satanic, and he flew into hysterical rages about trifles. Within the first few minutes of our meeting he made it clear that he despised Brennan and myself and proposed to have as little as possible to do with us. He was the eldest son of a Sligo land-owner, and had the natural contempt of the educated man for the self-educated. He under-valued his own education; I over-valued mine, and the laboriously acquired bits and scraps of Goethe, Heine, Musset and the Gaelic poets which with me passed for culture seemed to him mere country pedantry.

Our very first attempts to organize a library in Wicklow ran into bad trouble. Before the library committee had met at all, the priest who represented the Catholic Church on it told us that he intended to propose at our first meeting that the committee adjourn *sine die*. There would be no library at all if he could stop it, and he would. The reason for his opposition was still the fuss over Lennox Robinson's 'blasphemous story'. Although Robinson had been forced to resign and Tom McGreevy* had resigned with

* Robinson's assistant. He later became Director of the National Gallery, Dublin.

him, the entire library foundation came under suspicion. Clearly, the Carnegie United Kingdom Trust was involved in a vast conspiracy to deprive the poor Irishman of his faith.

Phibbs, an Irish Protestant with an English education, was incapable of understanding a situation like this, much less of dealing with it, and, left to himself, he would probably have delivered a few well-chosen blasphemies and retired in a huff. I knew that in Ireland you can oppose the clergy only with nationalists, so I introduced Phibbs to another ex-gaolbird, Seamus Keely, who taught Irish in the local technical school, studied law in his time off and was on his way to a judgeship.

Keely was a handsome man, though you could hardly see the good looks for the cloud of melancholy that surrounded him. Even the pince-nez on the end of his nose looked as if it were on the point of committing suicide. When I proposed that he should present himself at the committee meeting as a representative of the Carnegie United Kingdom Trust, he shrieked with outraged legal virtue; but when I explained that the alternative would be the abolition of the library, the humour of the suggestion dawned on him and he began to giggle. I also warned Phibbs, who would chair the meeting, to insist on a vote *ex officio*, which seemed to me a match for *sine die* any day of the week.

But it was not necessary. The mere presence of Keely, handsome, modest and fresh from an internment camp, and an exemplary Catholic besides, was enough to assure everyone that the Irishman's simple faith was in no immediate danger. I should add that afterwards Keely, the priest and I became great friends, but the Wicklow County Library owes its existence to a shameless piece of gerrymandering by an Irish judge who was probably even less ashamed of it than I was.

After that, Phibbs treated me with considerably more respect. What was more important from my point of view was that he showed his gratitude to Keely, though none of us knew that this gentle teacher of Irish would become a judge. Phibbs realized that in our ignorant way we knew things about Irish life that he had never been taught. It was the first time I realized the isolation of the Anglo-Irish, which Elizabeth Bowen once compared to the isolation of an only child. At home, all he had known of Irish literature was Miss Hutton's version of the *Cattle Raid of Cooley* – in which he had studied the youthful feats of Cú Chulainn, who drove a *sliotar* down the hound's throat and then beat it over the head with a hurley stick, and a patriotic novel by Canon Sheehan called *Lisheen*, which always lay on the living-room table, because the house was called 'Lisheen'. He began to sign himself 'Seathrún MacPhilip'. But he also had the Anglo-Irish incapacity for languages, and after attending a few of Keely's Irish lessons at the technical school, he resigned himself to monolingualism.

Phibbs became the dearest and best of my friends, and I have had many. I don't think I ever even showed Wilson a poem, but I showed all my work to Phibbs. He read my poems, which I hammered out on the office typewriter after hours, and marked them all 'Rubbish' except a few translations from the Irish, which I felt he excepted more because of the material than the treatment. He called for me each day at my lodgings on his way to work, but Mrs Soames soon stopped this. One day she came into the sitting-room, wailing and wringing her hands, and told me that she was delighted to welcome my friends at the house, but she had to make an exception of Mr Phibbs; he was the Devil. I told this extraordinary rigmarole to Phibbs, who was impressed rather than angry. He may have had a genuine interest in satanism and regarded her as a witch.

After this, we met at his rooms on the Murrough and drank small glasses of cheap sherry. He had a passion for the destructive criticism of religion, which I did not understand, and I still have his Bible with his exclamatory comments on the improbabilities and improprieties of the first few books – I doubt if he ever read further. He believed that marriage in the modern world was an outmoded institution. He forced Havelock Ellis's *Psychology of Sex* on me and was exasperated when I returned it unfinished and commented that it bored me. 'It is permissible to say one is shocked by such a book,' he said curtly. 'It is unforgivable to say one is bored.' He really enjoyed pornography, and when someone irritated him – which was often – he promptly got his own back by writing some murderous and bawdy satire. I still remember his poem on Robert Wilson's English wife:

> The night that she, just newly wed,
> Was brought, a blushing bride, to bed
> Hers was so stout a maidenhead
> That all his passion, all her will,
> Left her at dawn a virgin still ...

Yet I, who was so puritanical that I left a room rather than listen to dirty stories, never resented either his blasphemy or obscenity. I think I understood them as the play of a powerful and utterly fearless mind, and to me they were as interesting as the antics of a tiger. I was fascinated by the sheer mental agility that went with his physical agility, which was considerable. Despite his height he walked with short quick steps, changing step frequently to adjust himself to my own long, slow stride. Sometimes I just sat and watched him as though he were something in the zoo.

He had a sort of animal beauty and a touch of animal cruelty. He had been trained as a zoologist, but his only interest was poetry, and since he simply could not grasp the idea of a foreign language, this meant English poetry. He had joined the British Army as soon as he was old enough, but when a drill sergeant shouted at him: 'Hi, you! Take that damn thing out of your pocket!' he had shouted back with equal truculence, 'What do you mean, calling this book a damned thing? It's Shelley's *Collected Poems*.' If the war had continued, he would probably have made a very fine officer.

When he was self-conscious, as he usually was for the first quarter of an hour, particularly if there was someone else in the room, he was stiff, curt and mechanical; but when he relaxed he had all the grace of a thoroughbred. The long lanky hair hung over one eye; the thin lips softened, and you saw the thick, sensual lips of the poet, and he paced round the room with his hands in his trousers pockets, bubbling with boyish laughter. Later, when I read Proust, I knew exactly what Saint-Loup must have looked like.

He was an Irish country gentleman; so he regarded himself, and so he behaved – in the way in which an Irish country gentleman believes an English country gentleman behaves. He gave great thought to questions of precedence, and one night he asked me in great perturbation the meaning of a passage he had been reading in some eighteenth-century book, which laid it down that no gentleman sees his guest to the door. Being a boy from the Cork slums I had no difficulty in explaining to him that this is a butler's job, and this gave him much food for thought.

He loved poetry as no one else I have ever known loved it, and he rapidly turned me from a reader of anthologies into a reader of poetry – a very different thing. He loved all poetry, good and bad, famous and forgotten, but he loved the forgotten best, and would come triumphantly back to Wicklow with *Poems of Puncture* by Amanda McKitterick Ros or the works of Thomas Caulfield Irwin. He had an unerring eye for books, and he must have spent a small fortune on them. Once, in later life, he spotted the Kilmarnock edition of Burns on the shilling shelf and, true to character, instead of buying it he brought the error in valuation to the bookseller's attention. Once, maddened by people who borrowed books from him and did not give them back, he had defaced them all with a rubber stamp – 'This Book Has Been Stolen from Geoffrey Phibbs' – a typical, impulsive bit of vandalism that he must soon have regretted.

He read everything and studied everything that could conceivably have been called 'modern' or 'advanced': ballet, painting, sculpture, poetry and (even though he was tone-deaf) music. His favourite modern poet was an American woman of whom we were both to learn a great deal more. In reading, he preferred the difficult to the simple: it suited his agile, inquisitive mind, while I, of course, preferred the simple, above all if it was sufficiently gloomy. We were never in step: he loved bright modern pictures, Braque and Matisse, while I liked Rembrandt: he listened to Stravinsky or Bach on the gramophone, and I hummed the slow movement of the Beethoven C Sharp Minor Quartet; and when he quoted Carew:

To be a whore in spite of grace,
Good counsel, and an ugly face,
And to distribute still the pox
To men of wit. . . .

I replied with Landor's 'Artemidora, gods invisible . . .'

His own verse was comparatively straightforward, and he wrote
it every day – sometimes three or four poems at a time – and
always off the cuff, sometimes within an hour of whatever
incident had excited him. One evening, when we were out
walking on the hills over Wicklow, he killed a rat, and the poem
followed that very evening; another day, when he was alone, he
met Austin Clarke's wife, Margaret Lyster, and in due course, I
got the poem:

Mister Lyster
Gave it to me the day she had the blister
Between Jack's Hole and Five-Mile-Water
And introduced me to her landlord's daughter.

With him, verse was always immediate and spontaneous, and,
so far as I could see, complete. The pains and aches of composition,
which with me went on year after year, did not seem to exist for
him. We would be working together in the office and suddenly
he would reach out, grab an old envelope from the waste-paper
basket and begin to scribble furiously. Then he would go to the
typewriter and type it before he read it to me. I corrected the
spelling and grammar, a process that amused and exasperated
him: sometimes I thought he misspelled deliberately to keep me
occupied. 'You will die of sintactical exactniss of the mind,' he
once wrote to me. 'I believe it is a very slow and paneful death.'

Nowadays I wonder if those early poems were not much better
than I thought them. Now, at least, I realize how brilliant he was,
but then, with my large appetite for melancholy music, I thought
the poems too flashy, too topical and, above all, too slapdash; and
I longed for the moment when the wit and topicality collapsed
and let through the pure lyric tone:

Now lets laburnum loose all her light golden locks –

Or –

O solemn slope of mighty limbs so long accustomed to Arcadian
rams!
'But I'm not much of an antiquary,' she said. 'Oh, no,' I said,
'you're still quite young and nice.'

It doesn't matter. We were two young poets in love with our
trade, and though I wasn't a real poet I enjoyed it as though I
were, and not even one's first experience of love-making is quite
as satisfying as that.

4

THANKS to my friendship with Phibbs my position in life suddenly changed for the better. I had to borrow the library bicycle one night each week to cycle seven miles out into the mountains and teach Irish for the sake of the five shillings. My pupil was an old schoolteacher who had to learn Irish to keep his job; he was a kind old man and always saw that I had drunk well before he sent me home. But Phibbs grew very angry when he understood at last how hard up I was, and he wrote a cruel and witty letter to the Carnegie Trust about it. The Secretary replied handsomely by return, apologizing for Lennox Robinson's meanness, increasing my salary to two pounds ten a week and promising a further increase to three pounds ten when the Trustees met.

Even in Big Business overnight increases of more than a hundred per cent do not often occur, and when they do they do not involve the same distinction between poverty and wealth. I became reckless, and when I went home on holiday got my aunt's husband, Pat Hanlon, to make me a suit – the first I had owned since I was a small boy – and a shirtmaker to make me two green shirts. These were a tribute to Phibbs, who, as a serious poet, always wore green shirts and a black bow-tie. The problem of how to get a broad-brimmed hat like his had to be deferred till I reached a country where poets were respected and hats made to suit them, but I opened an account at Bumpus of Oxford and ordered a pocket Dante and a pocket Landor. The Dante was my own long-cherished wish, but the Landor was pure Phibbs.

Naturally I agreed to sign with him a manifesto against Yeats, to whom he had a great aversion, first because the Yeatses had been 'in trade', and second because Yeats (who, as I later realized, was half blind and had offended half Dublin by trying to be polite and call people by their names) had addressed him as 'Coulter'. George Russell, the Editor of the *Irish Statesman*, made some slighting reference to our manifesto, and Phibbs and I called to protest. Russell did his editing from an attic room in a Georgian house in Merrion Square, which he had papered in brown wrapping-paper and decorated with gods and goddesses in dark browns and gold. He sat behind a large desk to the side of the fireplace – a big, burly north of Ireland Presbyterian with wild hair and beard and a pipe hanging from his discoloured teeth. He usually sat well back in his chair, beaming benevolently through his spectacles, his legs crossed, and his socks hanging down over his ankles. Sometimes in an earnest mood he leaned forward with his two fat hands on his knees, his head lowered as he looked at you over the specs, giving his appearance almost an elfin quality. He was an extraordinarily restless, fidgety man, for ever jumping up to find some poem he was about to print (usually lost in the heap of papers, prints and manuscripts in his desk) or some book he was reviewing. With him was his secretary, Susan Mitchell, a deaf woman with a sweet, faded face, who was supposed to have loved him platonically for the best part of her life.

Phibbs, like many of the younger writers, despised Russell, whom he regarded as an old windbag. I was prepared to do the same, but, while we were still arguing, Phibbs said, 'The difference between your generation and ours is that we have had no youth.' 'Oh, really!' Russell replied with an air of great concern, and I disgraced myself by a roar of laughter in which Russell joined. One of his favourite quotations was a phrase from the *Three Musketeers* – 'I perceive if we do not kill one another we shall be good friends'; and I think at that moment Russell and I decided we should be friends, for as we were leaving he put his arm round my shoulder and said, 'Send me something for the paper.'

I did, and he printed it, and another source of income became open to me. Admittedly it was small, but when one has never had anything the occasional guinea or two guineas seems like wealth. I could now spend a night in a hotel – though six and sixpence for bed and breakfast struck me as wicked – so I went to Dublin, mastered even my timidity, and visited him in his house in Rathgar on Sunday evening. I went through the performance I went through so often in later years, climbed the steps, pulled the bell, heard the smelly old dog begin to yelp; and then Russell, shouting and kicking excitedly at the dog, pulled me in by the hand. He had the usual Dublin combination of living- and dining-room, filled with paintings, mostly by himself, and all in glaring colours that matched the glaring overhead light. Corkery, who had once visited him, had told me that the pictures were 'like Hampstead Heath on Sunday night'.

For the first hour he sat uneasily in his big chair in the middle of the room, intent on the doorbell, which was always anticipated by the infernal dog. It was like sitting in the middle of Grand Central Station. Visitors to Dublin – Americans, Japanese and Chinese – were always dropping in, as well as a gang of adoring old ladies whom I called 'The Holy Women'. He lectured to them all, telling American agriculturists how to organize co-operatives and Indians how to understand Gandhi, and suggesting new themes to poets and story-tellers. He talked in set patterns and phrases which had endured for years, some indeed of which could be traced back to his boyhood.

'You know, A.E.,' I said to him years later, 'back in 1904 Joyce has you saying: "The only question about a work of art is, out of how deep a life does it spring." '

'Well, that's clever of him,' Russell replied. 'That's true, you know. I may have said that.'

He said it at least once a day. What was more he did not realize that I was joking him.

He was a creature of habit, and his conversation, like his life, like his pictures, ran in patterns; well-formed phrases, ideas, quotations and anecdotes that he repeated year after year without altering an inflection. He was unskilful in the way he introduced them, and they were usually so general in their application that they had a tendency to obliterate the point in discussion. 'Leonardo advised young painters to study the stains in old marble to discover compositions for their own paintings' was a standard phrase that was exceedingly difficult to relate to any subject one was considering. After a time you got to see Leonardo hovering in the air a mile off and found yourself trying to ward him off as if he were a wasp.

It was this repetitiousness that got him the reputation of a windbag among people like Phibbs, and I understood the criticism even when I disagreed with it. In fact, Russell was a man of intense intellectual vitality; ideas came to him almost too readily, and his experience, when he chose to draw on it, was profound and varied, particularly when he remembered it casually as a result of something someone had just said and it came to him with the freshness of a theme rediscovered.

When the occasional visitors left to catch the last tram, and two or three regular ones like Osborn Bergin the philologist and C. P. Curran the lawyer remained behind, Russell ruffled out his beard as though he were expelling the smoke of generalization from it, and the talk – political and literary gossip – improved enormously. When we rose to go Russell cried, 'Oh, books! You must have books!' On the left-hand side of the wall between sitting- and dining-room there was a tall shelf of religious books that no one was allowed to borrow; but a big, low bookcase against the wall beside it was free to everybody. Russell, a poor boy himself, had picked up an occasional book in a second-hand store and made his soul on it, learning whole pages by heart (his verbal memory was fabulous), and he knew everyone must love books as he did. He would squat cross-legged before the bookcase, grab a new book and lift his glasses to read from it, his short-sighted eyes skipping from line to line, and then look up at you happily, drooling and beaming.

'Isn't that good? Isn't that clever? Don't you like that? Doesn't he interest you? Ah, but here's something you will like.'

I don't think I ever left that house or the office without an armful of books, good, bad and indifferent, and later, when I was in hospital, Russell continued to send me regular parcels of them – 'to raise your soul above the troubles of the flesh' as he would explain.

He was that sort of man. Within half an hour he enveloped you in universal curiosity and affection in which shyness was forgotten. It was like an old fur coat, a little bit smelly and definitely designed for someone of nobler stature, but, though it might threaten you with suffocation, it never left you feeling cold. He would find you a new doctor, a new wife, a new lodging or a new job, and if you were ill would cheerfully come and nurse you.

I did not quarrel with friends like Phibbs who resented the old fur coat, but I, who found it hard enough to write a letter and almost impossible to wrap up a parcel, appreciated the fury of affection that went into all that vague letter-writing, picture-giving and parcel-sending. It all came out of a great emotional abundance like that of one of the nineteenth-century writers he loved so much – Hugo or Dumas – and it was always a mystery to me how that emotional volcano poured forth only little twelve-line lyrics in which every second word was vague and literary.

As all Russell's discoveries had to be pronounced on by Yeats, Russell ordered me to visit him on one of his Monday evenings. In those days Sunday was Russell's night, Monday Yeats', Tuesday afternoon Sarah Purser's, Sunday afternoon Seamus O'Sullivan's. Yeats' Mondays were peculiar because they were all male; on Monday nights he discussed sex, except when Lady Gregory was staying, and, of course, it would be my rotten luck to be ordered to the presence when she was staying and no one else came, so that I had to face Yeats and herself alone. At that time I did not know Mrs Yeats, who could manage to make even me feel at home. To complete my confusion, Lady Gregory wore a mantilla as though for an audience with the Pope.

It was all too much for a raw youth who was terrified of social occasions anyhow. Yeats' study was kept deliberately dark, and everything in it was expensive and beautiful; the masks from his dance plays, the tall bookcases with the complete sets of the classics, and the long, orderly table with the tall silver candlesticks.

Even Corkery could not have said that the pictures were 'like Hampstead Heath on Sunday evening'. And nothing less like Russell could be imagined than the tall man in the well-cut blue suit with the silk shirt and bow-tie who came shuffling in, holding his hand out high as though he expected you to kiss his ring – a beautiful ring, as it happened. Never could you imagine an Irish country-man giving Yeats an approving look and shouting, 'Bring in the whiskey now, Mary, and be *continually* bringing in the hot water', which was how Russell was received in one Irish town. Later, the very sight of Yeats at the door would send Mother scuttling to her bedroom. There was something ecclesiastical about the blind man's stare, the ceremonial washing of the hands and the languid unction of the voice. That night I noticed that he said 'weld' and 'midder' for 'world' and 'murder'.

There was a touch of the bird about him as well; the eyes, like those of a bird, seemed to be at the sides rather than the front of the face, and his laugh tended to be harsh, abrupt and remote – a caw, as Moore called it. When he was happy and forgot himself, animation seemed to flow over him. He sat forward, arms on his knees, washing his hands over and over, the pose sometimes broken by a loud, harsh, throaty laugh and the tossing back of the big bird's head while he sat bolt upright in his chair gripping his lapels and raising his brows with a triumphant stare; sometimes he broke it by tweaking his nose; most characteristically perhaps by raising his index finger for attention. But when he was really excited his whole face lit up as from a light inside. It was astonishing, because even in old age when he was looking most wretched and discontented that blaze of excitement would sweep over his face like a glory, like a blast of sunlight over a moor, and from behind the mask a boy's tense eager face looked out at you. I had already noticed with Lennox Robinson the way you could see under the mask to the boy beneath. In Robinson the boy was a practical joker; a brat who had already done something terrible to your bed; but the boy behind Yeats' mask was one who had been kept in on a summer day and looked at you, trapped and despairing, from his bedroom window.

It was a while before I realized that Yeats was a desperately shy man who had the effect of driving other shy people slightly dotty as he drove me that night and many a night after. I am not saying that Russell was not shy – poets, after all, are not made of brass – but shyness was forgotten in the folds of the old fur coat, which, I fancy, was the thing about him that Yeats hated most. To Yeats, Russell was as much mob as man. Yeats loved the half light, Russell the full light, though Yeats was an infinitely more observant man than Russell; and if you had the misfortune to bore him you were perfectly well aware that he had marked you down as an enemy and would remember it against you in time to come.

In spite of the blindness, in spite of the shyness that made it impossible for Yeats to use Christian names, he was extra-ordinarily watchful and observant. Within the first half-hour George Russell would smother you with curiosity, affection and kindness, but I never felt that these bright, kind, honest eyes saw me at all; while Yeats, apparently blind, bored and bad-tempered, astonished me by his apparent familiarity with my life, my work and my friends.

'I know Strong is a great friend of yours, O'Connor,' he said one night many years later, 'but he *bores* me.'

The important thing to me was not that Strong bored him, but that he remembered that Strong was a friend of mine and was quite ready for an argument. On another night he said, 'I see the Censorship Board has banned the book by So-and-So – the fellow who stole your story.' I didn't know that anyone had stolen that particular story;* it has been stolen so often since that even the newspapers comment on it, but Yeats was the very first to notice the plagiarism.

There was no doubt as to which was the easier to make friends with, Russell or Yeats. That first night Lady Gregory and himself were putting me through my paces. Lady Gregory asked me to say some modern Irish poem, and I said Father Paddy Browne's translation of a poem of Gogarty's, which is better than the original. Then I spoiled it all by telling how another travelling

* 'Guests of the Nation'.

teacher of Irish like myself – Dick Murphy – whose small salary often went unpaid, tried to eke it out by producing his own translation of Lady Gregory's *Workhouse Ward*, but, being too poor to pay the royalties, re-titled it *Crime and Punishment. Translated from the Original Russian of Fyodor Dostoevsky*. I know it was not a tactful story to tell before the author, but I was embarrassed, and anyhow I still like 'from the Original Russian'.

'And didn't he know it was wrong?' Lady Gregory asked bleakly, in that flat, peasant accent of hers, and this ruined the rest of the evening for me.

It was no comfort to learn a few days later that Lady Gregory was re-telling the story all over Dublin or that Yeats had said my conversation was 'profound'. What I needed was that big, smelly old fur coat.

5

I WAS now comparatively well off, but the job of librarian in Cork County was coming up, and I dreamed of it. To my surprise Russell was violently opposed to my taking it at all. There were other jobs I could get within twenty or thirty miles of Dublin and he wanted me to apply for one of these: then I should be on the spot if a job turned up in Dublin itself, and meanwhile could spend my week-ends in town. He simply could not understand that I did not particularly want to live in Dublin, and he had the lowest view of Cork.

'My dear fellow,' he said dogmatically, 'you wouldn't be able to stand that hole for six months.'

What astonishes me now, looking back on the period, is that I did not even understand what he was getting at. Is it that young writers have no sense of fear? I was prudent enough. When I used the pseudonym 'Frank O'Connor' (my second name and my mother's maiden name) I left myself a loophole against the sort of mistake Lennox Robinson had made when he published his silly little story under his own name while still Secretary of the Irish Carnegie United Kingdom Trust, but the real dangers I did not see at all, then or for years after. Cork was to me merely my material, the place I knew best, and it never occurred to me that that particular material could ever have any effect on me, or that I might eventually find myself in the position of Heine's monkey chewing his own tail – 'Objectively he is eating, subjectively he is being eaten.'

And yet, during my time in Wicklow, I could see the consequences of this restrictiveness all round me. There was the problem of getting local sanction to establish our libraries, which was not made any easier by Robinson's 'crime'. Some of the priests would allow no libraries at all. In Rathdrum, a town up the country from us, the parish priest initially resisted all our efforts to start a branch library. At last I decided that the time had come to visit him. Phibbs and I called first on the curate, a splendid young fellow who was in despair with the parish priest and with Ireland. A couple of nights a week he went off to the local technical school and took off his coat to practise carpentry so as to encourage the unemployed lads of the town to learn a trade, all to no purpose.

'You'll go up to that parochial house', he said, 'and see the old man at the table with his dinner gone cold and a volume of Thomas Aquinas propped up in front of him. And between you and me and the wall,' he added, 'Thomas Aquinas was a bloody old cod.'

We found the parish priest exactly as the curate had predicted, Aquinas and all, but there seemed to be nothing of the obscurantist about the delightful old man we met. On the contrary, when we introduced ourselves, he beamed and regretted that we hadn't come to lunch. He took a particular fancy to me because I spoke Irish, and he was devoted to Irish and Irish literature. In fact, one of his dearest friends had been George Moore. Poor George. Of course he had been greatly wronged in Ireland, where people did not understand his work, but George had been a really dear and good man.

I didn't, of course, believe for an instant that he had been friendly with George Moore, but if the illusion made him more tolerant of our business it was all right with me. But when I introduced the subject I saw at once what the curate had meant. Oh, libraries. Libraries, hm! Well, libraries, of course, were wonderful things in their own place, but town libraries were a great responsibility. It was all very well for sophisticated people like ourselves to read the works of dear George, but could we really thrust them into the hands of simple Irish townspeople?

I damn near told him that from the little I knew of simple Irish townspeople they could give us all odds, but I knew this would get us nowhere. Charm was the thing, and charm won us permission at last, but only if the curate took full responsibility and satisfied himself of the innocuousness of the books we sent out. Swift wondered how it was that every virtuous English bishop translated to Ireland was murdered on Hounslow Heath and his place taken by a highwayman, but I wondered what happened to those nice, broadminded young curates one met after they became parish priests.

Nevertheless I was beginning to suspect that as an authority on Irish ways I was a wash-out. And now I had another shock coming to me, because, as we left, the parish priest said to me, 'I know you'll be interested in this', and handed me a presentation copy of *The Untilled Field*, in Irish, with an affectionate inscription by George Moore.

'It's all very well for you, O'Donovan,' the travelling teacher said testily one night as were standing on top of the stairs together, holding our candles and speaking in low voices so as not to disturb the Soameses. 'You don't know what life in this country is like. I can keep it up for a few years more, but I know damn well the way I'm going to die. I'll be dodging up to the church three or four times a day to say a prayer, and looking at the other side of the street when I meet some old friend that might be a temptation to me.

'That's the way my father died, and my father was a very intelligent man. He was one of a crowd in Limerick, and none of them believed in anything either. One of them – a fellow called Cremin – went to the States. They were all very fond of him. But you know the sort of thing that happens. One by one they got married and settled down and went to Mass, and they were ashamed of their old friends too, the way I'll be.

'And then, long after, Cremin wrote to say he was coming home. He was after making a bit of money and he wanted to retire to Limerick. Father was delighted. He couldn't believe that the good old days weren't going to come back. They were all delighted; they all liked Cremin, so they arranged for a big car to take them to Queenstown and meet the liner.

'Well, Cremin came ashore as sprightly as ever. They'd arranged for a dinner at the Commodore, and they made speeches about Cremin and their youth, and he got up to reply, and, begod, didn't he drop dead across the table!

'They brought him home that night and buried him, and after the funeral Father invited a Redemptorist back to the house, and from that day till the day he died we were never without a priest in the house. And I tell you, O'Donovan, that's the way I'm going to die too. You mark my words!'

But why should I mark them when the very same thing was taking place under my eyes in the Soames household? Neither Mrs Soames nor her son was very pious. In fact, Mrs Soames was a most superior woman. I think she had been parlourmaid in some Wicklow big house and married the coachman. In spite of her rigmarole about Phibbs being the Devil, she had a good natural intelligence, and hers was the only Catholic lodging-house I ever knew that wasn't cluttered up with holy pictures and statues.

Then we had a Redemptorist mission in the town. The women's turn came first, and each night Mrs Soames hobbled off to the church and she confessed and communicated like everybody else. She was no zealot, but like any other woman she did not want to be different.

But before the women's mission ended at all it was clear that there was trouble in the house. From the sitting-room I could hear herself and Bill arguing in the kitchen, her voice shrill and querulous and Bill's deep and mournful. When she brought in my glass of milk she was full of complaints. Bill refused to go to the mission at all. According to himself – and, knowing Bill well, I believed it – he had done no harm to anyone and had nothing at all to confess. What harm could he do, cycling out at the crack of dawn, wet or fine, miles out in the country and only seeing Bridie for one evening a week? Besides, it was too bloody silly. That was more or less the way I felt myself, but Mrs Soames seemed to feel that it was a matter of maternal discipline and that he mustn't make a show of her before the town.

The night the men's mission opened I heard the row going on

in the kitchen. Bill, with his deep husky voice, sounded like a cow that was being driven to the knacker's. His mother scolded and hounded him out, and then watched from the front door to make sure he did not bolt down some lane to the quays.

I followed to see the fun, but it wasn't very funny. The Redemptorist had one of those thick pulpit voices that bellowed till it bounced and then dropped to an awed whisper. He described to us what he obviously thought was how Voltaire died, knowing he was damned, and screaming, screaming for the priest who never came. As I emerged from the church the town atheist approached me.

'How did you like God's representative telling those damned lies?' he hissed angrily.

'He probably believed them himself,' I said.

'He never read a line of Voltaire's in his life,' said the atheist in a fury.

Then I saw Bill, and his whole face was lit up.

'How did you like that, Bill?' I said.

'Finest bloody sermon I ever heard in my life,' Bill said enthusiastically. 'Aha, that fellow knows how to talk.'

For the rest of the week his mother had no trouble in getting Bill shaved and dressed for the show. As a disciplinarian she might have taken alarm at this, but we are always blind when our temperaments are rushing us to a crisis. Nothing dawned on the poor woman until Saturday night, when Bill came home and told her he was getting married at once. The priest had given him a terrible time in confession, and asked him what he meant – a grown man with a steady job – indulging in occasions of sin with poor Bridie for fifteen years. Finally he had threatened Bill with a terrible death – by drowning, no less, though how Bill could get drowned in his daily excursions to the farm was not clear. Down, down, down he could go, and then rise again for a moment with outstretched hands, gasping for air – Voltaire himself had nothing on Bill. After a dreadful fifteen minutes Bill had slunk out of the church, convinced that everyone was looking at him and blaming him for some terrible crime he had never committed.

At first Mrs Soames was her usual sarcastic self and asked whether he had told the priest that he only earned twelve shillings a week – it may have been fifteen or eighteen, but it was in that neighbourhood. Bill replied that he had and the priest had said it didn't matter. Only then did the immensity of the disaster become clear to Mrs Soames. Her Boy, whom she had looked after and bullied and defended from designing women, had slipped out of her hands into those of a priest, and not even the poor decent Kerry priest she could pin the blame on, but a nameless Redemptorist who was here today and gone tomorrow.

For hours I heard the voices going on in the kitchen and felt ashamed to pass them on my way up the stairs. Finally, when Bill had gone to bed, Mrs Soames came in with my glass of milk and wept and wrung her hands. She had met the fate of every strong-minded woman and found an adversary stronger than herself. When she had tried to talk to Bill about money, all he had been able to do was to cover his eyes and describe the horrors of drowning.

'And when I asked him how they would live, he said Bridie would have to go on working. And when the children start coming? I said, and all I could get out of him was "God will provide". He will, I hear! I know who'll do the providing, Mr O'Donovan. I will. I'll have to take them in, and give them your room, and then the children will come and I'll have to mind them as well.'

She left me in a state of distraction, and God knows I was sorry for her – the saddest woman who had ever done her duty by attending a Redemptorist mission. But I saw it from outside – my material, as you might call it. It never occurred to me that anything of the sort could happen to myself.

6

NOTWITHSTANDING Russell's forebodings, I accepted the job of librarian in Cork County with a salary of two hundred and fifty pounds a year.

It was great money; more than anyone in Harrington's Square had ever earned, so far as I knew. Indeed, I suspect that Father's imagination refused to grasp it at all, and that it only worried him. It even worried me at times, because I had more in common with Father than I liked to admit; but Mother, with her placid, sanguine temperament, knew it was the will of God and a proper reward for my years of hardship, so she rented a gas stove to cook properly and had gaslight installed in the kitchen and the front room so I could write without straining my eyes.

To furnish the front room she bought a second-hand carpet, a round table that was a little unsound on its one leg, two dining-room chairs and an armchair. I bought myself a Morris chair – a poor commercial substitute for the fine chair that Corkery had made for himself, a second-hand typewriter for seven pounds, a print of Degas dancers (as a student in the School of Art I had quarrelled with my teacher, who said that Degas could not paint, and later I quarrelled with Yeats about him), a gramophone and a few records of Mozart and Beethoven. I also got the local carpenter to make me a fitted bookcase that ran the length of one wall. As well as that I bought a black suit to go with the green shirts and the black bow-tie. 'We writers, ma'am', as Disraeli said to Queen Victoria.

But beyond this my imagination, which was strictly conditioned to the interior life, did not function too well. Indeed, it would not be too much to say that it did not function at all. Anyone with a glimmer of worldly wisdom would have bought himself a comfortable modern house with a bathroom; and indeed some glimmerings of this I must have had because Father and I argued over it for years.

He was an emotionally generous man and did not hold it against me that – so far, at least – I had not turned into the liability he had prophesied. Among his old comrades of the Munster Fusiliers it flattered him to see my name in the papers and know I was in a public job – pensionable, of course; anything else would be valueless. He even came to see the advantages in the gas stove and the aluminium kettle. He liked to get up early and make the tea. 'Star of Life's Ocean!' as Minnie Connolly said, 'if a man brought me up tea at seven in the morning I'd plaster him with it.'

All the same I suspect that he was never without a secret feeling that there was something flighty and insecure about it all, even about the gas stove; something that lacked the Roman calm and permanence of his own two military pensions and the reliable old iron kettle. With these a man knew where he was, so he advised caution. *If* I had a little bit of money over and above (between grown men he realized that neither of us could afford to admit anything of the kind or people would start trying to borrow it from us) the thing to do was to put it in the bank. And seeing how difficult I found it to dispose of my money in any practical way, the bit of me that was Father inclined to the same view.

Besides, he would add with great resignation, one of these days I should be wanting a home of my own. This again was an appeal to my non-existent manliness and a gentlemanly assumption that I was not in love with my mother. What would he and she do then? The picture of my throwing out the pair of them for the sake of any woman struck me as merely laughable, but he nodded his head gravely and assured me that Life was like that.

And when this argument was not enough he had a real clincher. The son of an old friend had become a famous boxer and had immediately bought his parents a fine house in the suburbs. Father and the boxer's father, who adored his son, met occasionally after Mass and went for long walks together, usually to some new building development on the outskirts of the city, but always ending up outside his friend's old house in the poorer part of the city where the old friend had lived when he was poor and innocent and happy; and his friend would say, 'God, Mick, I'd hate the Boy to know it, but I never had a day's happiness in that other bloody misfortunate hole!'

Anyhow, Father's reasons for not wanting to move went deeper than that – much deeper, and if I could plumb them I could reveal every detail of his character and much of my own. He didn't own our house; he had to pay four and sixpence a week for it; but he identified himself completely with it and would have died for it if necessary. Children playing ball outside his gate plagued him – they might break a window – and he would stand in ambush behind the lace curtains in the front room, watching them, while Mother sat in the kitchen, sewing or reading.

'Min!' he would whisper in a tone of high tragedy.

'Wisha, what is it now?'

'It's that little pup of the Horgans again!'

'Ah, wouldn't you forget them and read your paper?' Mother would ask in a complaining tone.

'How can I read my paper?' Father would hiss back. 'My goodness, what sort of parents do them children have?'

He was waiting for the supreme moment when one of them would jump over the wall from the next garden after his ball, or take a swing on the squeaky gate with the broken latch. Then he would rush to the front door, fling it open and glower and mutter at the children, who would run madly to the top or bottom of the Square and stand there, daring him. Father was too good a neighbour to make scenes that would involve him with the parents, and this left him in a permanent state of frustration, for after a couple of minutes of outraged dignity he would stamp back slowly to the kitchen, brooding on firing parties, the cat-o'-nine-tails and other neglected forms of military discipline.

At the same time though, like any true artist scornful of general criticism, he could admit to small weaknesses in his masterpiece and remedy them in his own way. When I pointed out that the wall and gate-pillars were disintegrating, he studied them at length with pursed lips, working out how they could be repaired at little or no expense. He had noticed a pile of quite good discarded bricks on some building site and brought brown-paper parcels of them home after dark, pleased as an old dog who has disinterred a juicy bone. Mother, accustomed to his treasure trove, gave them a curious eye and asked, 'What are you going to do with them?' 'You'll see,' Father said complacently. We saw. He knew a builder's labourer who could wangle him a bit of cement and some sand, and after evenings of labour during which trowel, cement and bricks had all turned and bitten him, he asked me to admire brand new gate-posts, not perpendicular, of course, and very rough on the top, but still substantial, and now if God would only throw in his way a latch he could mortar into it and prevent those ill-mannered kids from using his gate as a swing, we should have a better house than any on the College Road and for a mere four and six a week. Father's attitude to new building developments was mixed, to put it mildly. As a Corkman with a low opinion of all other nationalities, particularly Dubliners, he was fascinated by the expansion of the city, but as a potential victim he was highly critical of it.

So I could not have a house, and I was scared at the prospect of trying to keep a car in Harrington's Square – 'them kids' would take it asunder – but I was determined that at least I should rent a cottage by the sea for a few weeks in summer as others did. Father humoured me and even agreed to come down and join Mother and myself for a couple of days himself. Anything longer would be impossible, and even the couple of days involved something like preparations for a siege of the home. It was not enough that neighbours guaranteed to watch it; bolts and window fastenings had to be renewed and strengthened, and when he left the house the gate was tied to the gate-post with coils of barbed wire.

I enjoyed having him with us because he was an even better walker than myself, though a more perfunctory one. On a visit to the country his trained military eye sized up the number of roads, and he liked to inspect each once, and when the inspection was complete to go home. The fact that a road was attractive did not mean it needed a second inspection.

One of these walks in Courtmacsherry is very vivid in my memory, and I wrote a story about it long after. We had climbed a hill overlooking the sea, and on the horizon, apparently moving across it in a series of jerks, like the swan in *Lohengrin* was an American liner on its way into Cobh. A farmer working in a field by the road joined us; he too had been watching the liner and it had reminded him of his son who had emigrated to America when he was quite young. After a few years the boy had married an Irish-American girl whose family had come from Donegal, and soon after ceased to write home, though his wife continued to write. Then she fell ill and her doctor suggested a holiday in Ireland. She had arrived one day on a liner like the one we were watching, and her father-in-law had met her at the station with his horse and cart. She had stayed with them for weeks, regained her health and gradually won the affection of the family. After that she had set off to visit her parents' family in Donegal, and it was only then that the old Cork couple had learned from a letter to a neighbour that their son was dead before ever she left America.

Up there on the hill in the evening with the little whitewashed farmhouse beside us and the liner disappearing in the distance, it was an extraordinarily moving story, all the more so because the farmer was obviously still bewildered and upset by it.

'Why would she do a thing like that to us?' he asked. 'It wasn't that we weren't fond of her. We liked her, and we thought she liked us.'

Clearly he suspected that some motive of self-interest was involved, and I was afraid to tell him my own romantic notion that the girl might have liked them all too well and kept her husband alive in their minds as long as she could and – who knows? – perhaps kept him alive in her own.

I knew that some time I should have to write that story, but Father only listened with the polite and perfunctory smile that he gave to the scenery. Both, no doubt, were suitable for people living in backward places, but did not call for closer inspection, and next morning he was up at six to make sure of catching the noon bus for Cork.

He was the most complete townie I ever knew.

7

ONCE, summing up what she owed to Father, Mother said that since the day of their marriage he had never looked at the side of the road another woman walked on.

She was probably right. Father was a one-woman man, and in the same way he was a one-town man, and one might go even farther and say he was a one-house man. In some extraordinary way she and Cork and the house in Harrington's Square (not to mention the pensions) were all fused together into a vast complacency that hid whatever fundamental insecurity drove him to his terrible drinking bouts. Clearly I had something of his weakness to go back to Cork in defiance of Russell's warnings. Mother worried and fretted even more than I did, but I feel that inside she was quite free of the tyranny of objects, and I sometimes wonder if she was not half-suffocated by the close texture of Father's world – and my own.

It was pleasure enough for me to be back with money in my pocket among those, some of whom had regarded me as a half-wit and a ne'er-do-well and some who had wished me well and thought I had something in me if only I got a chance. Even Mother, ordinarily so humble, had her little moments of satisfaction, as when the ambitious woman who had refused to salute me when I was poor took her aside to ask if the books I was always reading when I was a boy were all about being a librarian. 'I didn't bother to enlighten her,' Mother said stiffly, knowing that poor Mickie Joe, the ambitious woman's son, would at once be sent to the library to borrow books on librarianship.

But I also had enough of Mother's intellectual inquisitiveness in me to make me aware within a month that Russell had been right.

I couldn't stand the damn place. It was one thing to be in exile from it, compelled to make friends of Phibbs and Russell and rely on brief visits to report on them to Jack Hendrick* and Corkery, and another thing entirely to be in Cork with Hendrick and Corkery, waiting for the post to bring me news of Phibbs and Russell. This was a reversal of parts which I hadn't expected at all, because it had simply never occurred to me that I could feel as deeply about new friends as about old ones. One night when I met Corkery in King Street, I said it to him quite innocently, and afterwards felt that things were never quite the same between us.

At last I was beginning to get a picture of Ireland, the real Ireland, lonely and dotty. This was no longer the romantic Ireland of the little cottages and the hunted men, but an Ireland where everyone was searching frantically for a pension or a job. I also found that my ability to handle a priest in County Wicklow was no qualification for handling the Cork County Council.

On my first morning at work I came to interview the Secretary of the County Council. I had a cheque in my pocket for what was to me a vast sum from the Carnegie United Kingdom Trust, and I needed instructions as to where I should lodge it. I had also to select premises for my library and insure them. Under such circumstances it was the business of the senior County Council official to advise, and it was our business to regard the advice as instructions. The final decision rested with the Library Committee of the County Council when it was formed, but it was also common form that the Committee should not interfere with the Council on whom they would eventually have to rely for funds.

But, of course, nothing like this happened to me. I knew my Turgenev and Tolstoy, but they were useless when applied to local authorities. What I needed was a strong dose of Gogol, an author whom I had never studied.

I arrived at the Secretary's office at ten o'clock in the morning and was told he was at Mass. This sort of message is one that every Irishman automatically accepts. The Secretary may even have been at Mass. About eleven-thirty he came strolling in, a tall,

* See *An Only Child*, ch. 15.

49

gangling man with long white hair and a white moustache and a wonderful air of inconsequent buccaneering. A number of people seemed to be waiting on him, and he shouted at one, became involved with another, and whatever the subject was he seemed to change it.

He did precisely the same thing with me. For the best part of half an hour I tried to get from him the instructions I would have got from the Secretary of the Wicklow County Council in five minutes, but every time he evaded me. Finally the Angelus bell rang from the Franciscan church behind the court-house, and he slowly clambered on to his desk – a tall, old-fashioned desk like a lectern – joined his hands and closed his eyes. When I interrupted him again, he snapped at me angrily.

'Ah, let me say my prayers!' he said. And that was all the advice I ever got from the Secretary of the Cork County Council. I doubt if even Gogol would have been enough.

I went from him straight to the manager of the County Council bank and modestly asked to be allowed to open an account with the large cheque in my pocket.

'When you produce a resolution signed by the chairman of your committee, Mr O'Donovan,' the manager said coldly, practically implying that I had stolen it.

I was distracted. Never in my life had I had a bank account or more money on a cheque than would pay my own small salary, but I did know that people deposited such cheques in a personal account, collected the interest and then later wrote a cheque for the original amount, and I was sure that sooner or later someone would accuse me of having stolen it. I knew one member of the County Council who had voted for my appointment, so I went to see him in his office in Patrick Street. He was a big fat man who had told me the story of his life – the publishable portions at least – when I went to solicit his vote, and I had liked him for it. As a boy his dream had been of becoming a great violinist, and he had practised in his room till he was found out and beaten by his mother.

Normally he moved slowly and apparently with great

difficulty, but he moved like a bird when I told him my sad story.

'Leave it to me, boy!' he said in a sad, booming voice. 'Leave it to me!'

He took me straight to his own bank and repeated the story to the manager. The manager, who obviously admired Mr Buckley, as I may call him, received me with Christian understanding and said there would be no difficulty; he would take it on himself; and when I left an account had been opened on behalf of the Carnegie United Kingdom Trust. I was very relieved and thanked my friend Mr Buckley. He told me that whenever I was in difficulty again I had only to call on him.

I suspect now that Mr Buckley knew very well the difficulty I was in and intended that I should remain in it. Before a week was over I had visits from a score of councillors who complained of my opening an account for a sub-committee of the County Council in an unauthorized bank. Obviously they did not believe my version of the incident.

By the time the County Council Secretary had done with organizing my sub-committee it consisted of a hundred and ten members, and anyone who has ever had to deal with a public body will realize the chaos this involved. Finally I managed to get my committee together in one of the large council rooms, and by a majority it approved my choice of bankers. There was, I admit, a great deal of heat. Some of the councillors felt I had acted in a very high-handed way, and one protested against my appearing in a green shirt – a thing which, he said, he would tolerate from nobody.

A general meeting of the County Council was being held at the same time in another part of the building. During the discussions I was exasperated by people banging on the doors at one side of the chamber we occupied.

Later I learned that (through an oversight, no doubt) all the doors leading into the committee-room from the Council Chamber had been locked, so that councillors who wished to oppose my choice of banker had been locked out and only those who knew the architecture of the building were in their seats on time.

By the time the next meeting was held the supporters of the County Council bank were staging a revolution. They accused me publicly of having had the doors of the committee-room locked so that they could not arrive at the meeting on time. I was out of my wits, trying to understand. Several councillors tried to explain to me, but I didn't understand their explanations. 'You see,' one would say in a whisper, 'poor Murphy has an overdraft in the Banba Bank', but I did not see why that should make him so angry with me. Another said that 'Buckley is under the thumb of the Eire Bank', but that did not make any sense to me either. It was all very confusing.

By that time other events had me more nonplussed than ever. The manager of the insurance company that handled the Council's business had called. He was a very nice man, and he made no objection at all to insuring the library premises and stock. Here at last, I felt, was a really sensible man. But a week or two later I received by post a substantial cheque from the insurance company, and it was made out to me personally. I telephoned and was assured that it was perfectly all right. This was the commission on the insurance, and it was correctly made out to me. When I suggested that it should be made out to the Secretary of the Cork County Library Committee, the manager hastily said he would come over and explain it to me.

I have said he was a nice man, and he did his best for half an hour to make things clear to me, but that day I was denser than usual. The one thing I did gather was that the insurance company could not make out the cheque so that it could be lodged to the credit of the committee because this would be a great embarrassment to other officials. Considering the amount of property that other officials had to insure compared with the library premises, I saw that this might be so, but it didn't help me about what I was to do with the cheque. The damn thing pursued me for years, and so did the insurance company, begging me either to cash the cheque or give it back. When I left the public service for ever twelve years later I still had it with me.

I really should have studied Gogol.

But if I didn't know what was going on, other people did, or at least affected to do so. There was a small but determined group of old-fashioned Republicans on the Council which did its damnedest to have the Secretary fired, but whenever the battle was pitched the Secretary always won. I saw him at work myself, and his technique was fantastic. He could be dignified. When that failed he could clown, and there is nothing that the majority of men prefer to a clown. When the hunt became too fierce he would grab at a pile of correspondence and say, 'Gentlemen, in connection with what we are discussing, I have before me at this minute a letter from the Minister of Local Government', and then proceed to read a letter which dealt with drainage in Ballymorebingham, and before anyone knew what was happening the representative from Ballymorebingham would be on his feet, denouncing the Department of Local Government and taking the heat off the Secretary, who sat listening with an attentive air.

Then there was the County Council clerk, a small, gentle, inoffensive man, who had appointed himself Grand Inquisitor of the Cork County Council. 'I watch everything they do, Mr O'Donovan. Someone must clean out the Augean stables.' Once a small businessman rang me up to ask when his account would be paid, and I replied that it had already been approved for payment a month before and sent to the Secretary for endorsement. He asked if I couldn't get it speeded up, and I asked what the difficulty was in collecting it. He said in that hopeless Irish voice, 'Look, I'd better come round and explain it to you' – exactly as the insurance man had said. He came round to see me and I liked him at once, though I didn't know what he was talking about. He said that in order to get his cheque he would have to give somebody a hand-out. I didn't know what he was talking about even then, and enquired why. He replied that every shopkeeper in Cork had to do it. At this I lost my temper and said I would ring up the Secretary's office, and if his account was not paid within a week I would report the matter direct to the Department of Local Government. For a while he looked at me incredulously, and then he said, 'Mr O'Donovan, if you could do that you would have every small shopkeeper in Cork on his knees before you.' I did not have to do it, because immediately after my first telephone call the account was paid, so I never had the spectacle of the small shopkeepers of Cork on their knees before me to contemplate.

So naturally I didn't pay too much attention to the little clerk, though he always managed somehow or other to meet me outside the office with fresh denunciations and fresh threats of reporting it all to the Minister. Perhaps it was just as well that I hadn't had to protest to the Minister myself, for when the little clerk did report direct to the Minister for Local Government, he was promptly dismissed by sealed order. Left in middle age with nothing, the Grand Inquisitor set out for Dublin to live with his sister and devote his gentle, God-fearing life to showing up the Minister. When I moved to Dublin myself, he came along regularly to tell me how his great case against the Minister was going. Usually he came when I finished work and walked home with me, the happiest man in the world because he was sacrificing himself for the only thing he cared about – France. 'Ever since I was a boy I have loved France', he would proclaim dramatically, stopping on the pavement and beaming at me. It was France he was dreaming of when he tried to tidy up the tangled affairs of the Cork County Council, France he was dreaming of when he switched his attention to the whole country.

I sometimes wanted to hug him as he trotted along beside me with his glowing face, happy and doomed. For I, too, wanted to do something about the country.

When at last I had got the Library organized I realized that I had to have closer contact with the country branches. I bought a van to carry the book boxes about – I did not realize the necessity for a proper travelling library until this was under way – and Cronin, my assistant, and myself drove all over the county in it. This was another eye-opener. It made me realize that I was a townie and would never be anything else. In the best of the houses I visited – usually the houses of people who had been prominent in the Troubles – the people were better related to the wild country about them than I was to the tame city about me. Seeing them in

Cork in their uncouth clothes with their uncouth accents was one thing; seeing them on their own farms was another thing entirely, and it made me conscious of my own uncouthness rather than theirs. But those families were few, and the total effect of the country on me was one of depression.

It was as much to escape from the unreality of my work as for any other reason that I started a dramatic society in the city. There had been no such thing since Corkery had organized his little theatre twenty years before. There was the Cork Operatic Society, which in the usual way of provincial societies performed a Gilbert and Sullivan opera once or twice a year, with the aid of an English producer. There was also a local Shakespearean Society, run by a priest, which performed Shakespeare with the dirty words left out. We held our drama meetings in the old Women's Prison where Sean Neeson gave us space.

I knew even less about the theatre than I did about being a librarian, but I read and re-read every textbook on the subject and learned how to make scenery and organize the lighting – that is, if you could get a proper lighting set, which I never could, so that even today the one part of a production which I shall have nothing to do with is the lighting.

Our first production was to be Lennox Robinson's *Round Table* – one of his functional comedies, which could be transferred to an English provincial production by the change of a few town-names – his personal names were strictly inter-racial. I found suitable actresses very hard to get. The heroine is a determined, bossy type, but that type seemed to be quite unknown in Ireland. The moment you put an Irish girl on the stage and told her to say: 'Now, have you all washed your hands?' she instantly realized that there was something slightly improper about addressing men in this tone and became either coy or wheedling. I did it for them, but that only made them more embarrassed than ever, and they became practically tearful. I had just decided to give it up as a bad job when someone tapped me on the shoulder. It was a good-looking girl with an atrocious stammer. 'W-w-w-would you m-m-m-m-mind t-terribly if I t-t-tried that part', she asked with a determined air. I decided that she was pulling my leg and said without looking round, 'Well, you can't be any worse than the one that's doing it.' She got up and did it as though all her life she had been doing nothing else. Nancy McCarthy became my leading actress.

After this we produced *The Cherry Orchard*. I think I had been toying with *The Playboy of the Western World* because either then or soon afterwards we rehearsed it, but the results were too horrible. I realized during these rehearsals that a writer writes not only for a particular group; he writes for a particular accent. Everybody in Dublin suffers from adenoids, so Synge had no difficulty in finding actors who could sustain a long, unbroken line through speeches in the manner of Racine, but the Cork accent goes up and down, up and down, and I could find no actor or actress who could sustain a note even during a brief speech.

I had to be content with naturalism, and even naturalism involved me in difficulties. One of the lessons I learned during *The Cherry Orchard* production was that my translation of the Russian names had not taken me far enough into the whole business of theatre. There were 'versts' and 'roubles', and, just as I did not know from my training as a librarian that the one thing I needed was to get into immediate communication with my readers, so as a budding man of the theatre I didn't know that there is no way of getting an actor to say 'verst' or 'rouble' as though he knew exactly what it meant, nor is there any way of making contact with the audience except through its own knowledge of life. I saw it all quite clearly in that wonderful scene of the two sisters chattering in the dawn with the shepherd's pipe sounding in the distance. The only trouble was that I had no method of making a sound like a shepherd's pipe or, even if I had, of getting an audience to identify it as a shepherd's pipe. I could not believe but that I could master that pipe and give the same unearthly effect to a Cork audience that it must have had for a Russian one. I still did not realize what I was to argue later, against Yeats and everyone else in Dublin, that theatre is a collaboration between author, actors and audience, and when that collaboration ceases to exist, theatre ceases to exist.

It is clear I didn't recognize it then, because I went on with *A Doll's House*. But from other things I was beginning to realize that Cork standards of literature and my own could not exist for long side by side. I had got a hint of this when our Ranevskaya confessed she couldn't say the line 'At your age you should have a mistress'. Then the young newspaperman who was playing the part of Firs supported her with his own argument. This was that, as the nephew of the Dean, he could not possibly tolerate such a line being spoken. I should have given up at that point, because the priest who conducted the Shakespearean Society was also attacking us in print and complaining that instead of the uplifting plays of Shakespeare we wanted to produce the filthy work of Seán O'Casey. As a result our leading man failed to turn up at the dress rehearsal. He sent a message that he had a toothache, and when one of the group went to his lodgings, it seemed that the toothache was so bad that he couldn't come to the first night either. Hendrick had to postpone the show until Tuesday and that night he and Nancy worked for hours trying to teach me the part.

In those couple of years I published two or three stories, one of them, 'Guests of the Nation', in the *Atlantic Monthly*. Nevertheless, as I have said, I did not enjoy my years in Cork, because it was no longer the place I had known. O'Faolain was in America and I found it impossible to talk to Corkery. He was too gentle and considerate to be rude, but he made it plain that he was taking sides and that I was on the wrong one. I was restless and felt that Cork was threatening to suffocate me. I suffered from a sort of intellectual schizophrenia, living for the few days in the year when I could get up to Wicklow, talk literature and art to the Phibbses, and go on to Dublin and see Russell and Yeats. Russell could give me all the latest books and gossip, and of a Sunday evening I could go to the Abbey Theatre, where the Dublin Drama League was putting on a remarkable series of continental plays, Chekhov, Strindberg and contemporary German plays in which Phibbs' friend, Denis Johnston, was a leading figure.

I had also fallen in love in a completely hopeless way with my leading lady in the dramatic society. I had been reading Chekhov's love letters to Olga Knipper and probably felt I needed an actress of my own. Nancy was not in the least like Knipper. She was a pharmacist and very conscious of her responsibilities, and as well as that she was a very pious Catholic. When people complained of prescriptions she went to S. Peter and Paul's to pray. When they took legal proceedings she made a novena. For a year or more I always seemed to be meeting that girl outside S. Peter and Paul's. I gave her Chekhov's letters to Knipper, but they seemed to have no effect. She just wouldn't marry me.

Even so, when I applied for a job as municipal librarian in Dublin, I still had the notion that I should do it only as a temporary expedient until a similar job turned up in Cork. Nothing could cure me of the notion that Cork needed me and that I needed Cork. Nothing but death can, I fear, ever cure me of it.

PART TWO

THE PROVINCIAL
IN DUBLIN

8

I HAD been ill in Cork, and Russell, distrusting all Cork people, including doctors, had made me come to Dublin and get examined by his own doctor, Frank Purser, the only medical man he trusted. 'He cured Stephens. Stephens was dying when Frank saw him first, and now he can eat beef-steaks.'

When Russell heard that a new appointment was to be made in Dublin, he went wild and besieged a couple of government departments, assuring them that I was the only possible candidate, though whether this did me good or harm I never knew. But I got the job – organizing the library at Pembroke. When I saw the new library I was to work in, I cursed. It was a miniature Georgian version of a Dublin library of 1880, which in its turn had been copied from some English library of 1840.

Pembroke, like Rathmines, was one of the old townships that disappeared a few years later in Dublin city; it had a substantial Protestant population, and I found myself with a committee which was neatly balanced, but small enough to be practical. I made my first friend in a boy who came to me looking for a job, supported by the local Labour Party. I sent him to see my chairman, who ran an automobile business in Dublin. 'But don't you realize that he's a Freemason?' the boy asked. 'Never mind what he is', I said. 'I want him to support you when the committee meets.' He went off in the spirit of the Light Brigade, but next day the 'Freemason' came in and said, 'I thought that was a fine lad you sent to see me yesterday. He's getting my vote.' He did get the chairman's support, which was just as well for me and the library, as the Labour vote happened to go elsewhere. By a bare majority vote Dermot Foley became my assistant.

After Cork it was wonderful. Dermot was a musician, and we built up a music library that we could be proud of. I was a language enthusiast, and we built up a foreign library which attracted those French, Germans and Italians in Dublin who could find nothing in their local libraries. We bought an epidiascope and a cheap gramophone, and each week we talked to the children about pictures and classical music until the Dublin Corporation took over, removed our epidiascope and gramophone and sent Gaelic League lecturers who talked about Red Hugh O'Donnell and life in the Gaeltacht until they drove the kids away.

I had a room in Sandymount Green in a big house kept by a Donegal man and his sister who had retired to enjoy themselves in the great city. I do not think they enjoyed themselves much, because all their talk was of Donegal. I was never much in love with Dublin, but I thought they were unfair to it and said so.

'Ah, but you still have your dreams, Mr O'Donovan,' said the sister, her eyes filling with tears.

I liked them, but I adored my fellow lodger. He was an engineer, tall and dark and handsome, with grave manners and an enchanting smile. He was a saint as Mother and Minnie Connolly were saints, but a masculine version of the type.

I am a heavy sleeper, and I had an arrangement with him to wake me each morning on his way to Mass, but I slept so heavily and he woke me so gently, touching me with his fingers and then smiling into my face to reassure me, as one wakes a baby, that I did exactly what a sensible baby would do and went off to sleep again.

This caused him great scruples of conscience, because he had trained himself to leap out of bed at the first sound of the alarm clock by imagining that the bed was on fire. He was now training himself to wake immediately *before* the alarm clock went off, which he assured me was not so difficult as it sounded; and he felt sure that by waking me in this childish manner he was sapping my will power. Everybody, from Corkery on, seemed to be concerned about my will power.

He then made me prepare a card reading 'Please Wake Me at 7.30', which I had to hang on the door-handle before going to bed. He said that this made all the difference between a real act of the will and an automatic gesture, but I could not see that it improved my character in the least. All that really happened was that I usually forgot to hang it up.

Everything in the Saint's life had been reduced to schedule, even the walk from Sandymount Green to the Star of the Sea church, which was so many hundred steps and took so many minutes and seconds, measured by the watch on which everything was tested – exactly the complaint that a writer of the early Middle Ages makes of the Irish monks and their arithmetical piety. When we went for walks, I was a sore trial because I stopped to speak to anyone I knew, but those foolish, social conversations interrupted the flow of the Saint's thought, and he walked on to the next corner. Waiting for me while I chattered worldly irrelevancies was almost as bad as listening to them, because it threw out the whole mathematical quality of the walk, and after a while he explained to me that he would continue his walk at exactly the same pace – so many steps to the minute – and by quickening my own pace slightly, say by three steps to the minute – I could easily catch up on him. Running, of course, he neither expected nor approved of. Running and thinking were incompatible.

Any money left over from his rather good salary was available without interest to anyone who wanted it, and as I was short of money during the first few months of my stay in Dublin, I borrowed from him as well. But he was always getting into trouble because so few of the people who borrowed from him paid him back at the promised time, and sometimes new borrowers appealed to him when he himself was short.

No watch could control this, and once he came to me in great distress. I owed him a couple of pounds which I should pay when I got my first month's salary, and someone had asked him for money in a hurry at a time when he did not have it. He came to my room, blushing, and asked if I could lend him a pound that evening. If I could he promised to pay it back when he got his own pay on Friday night. At first I thought he was joking and laughed, and this distressed him even more. He swore that only dire need could make him borrow from a friend like myself, and then I realized that he was really in earnest, so I only laughed louder than ever, while he went through every gambit of the confirmed panhandler; and the more he tried to persuade me that he was not the sort of person who normally did this, and that he really would pay me back on Friday, the louder I laughed. Nobody else had ever made me laugh so much or with so good a conscience.

But no more than Mother or Minnie Connolly was the Saint anyone's fool. Like them he was simply a person of spiritual genius who treated money in the proper way. He was always in trouble with his infernal Loan Office, and one day he came to me with a circular which he was proposing to send to all his ancient debtors. It ran something like this, though I suspect the original was much subtler and funnier:

Dear —— , I don't know if you will remember that on . . . 19.. you borrowed from me the sum of . . . This letter is not intended as a request for payment, but it would help my book-keeping if you would kindly reply to two questions –
      (a) Do you acknowledge the debt?
           and
      (b) Do you propose to repay it?

It was the most effective dunning letter I had seen, and I am sure the money came pouring in, but the Saint could get his own back on me in exactly the same gentle, subtle way. He kept on trying to persuade me to come to Mass with him, and was not in the least concerned when he did not succeed. God, he explained, knew that I was a very good Catholic – even if I did not know it myself – and would accept a reasonable compromise. So the Saint went to two Masses on Sunday, one for himself and one for me, and on the second occasion explained to God that he was representing me.

This was moral blackmail, but he went one better. He decided that, as one of the few really good Catholics he knew, I should contribute to the Society for the Propagation of the Faith, a cause in which I had no interest whatever. We had a thundering row about this in which I accused him of every form of complacency and arrogance, but he won, as usual. He explained quietly that God, knowing me as He did, expected me to contribute to the Society for the Propagation of the Faith, so he would add my subscription to his own.

What can you do with a saint? Heine once said that the Celts were the only real believers because you could borrow money from a Celtic money-lender and arrange to pay it back in the next life. Maybe in the next life I shall pay back what I owe the Saint, including my subscription to the Society for the Propagation of the Faith – blast it!

But sanctity was not the origin of the trouble I was having with my other dear friend. When he was an assistant like myself, Phibbs had fallen in love with another assistant, whom he had wanted to marry, but since then he had fallen in love with a Dublin painter. It is not an unheard of situation among poets and, indeed, among others.

He and I had been coming back from a long walk over the hills by Rathnew when he told me. He might have chosen a more experienced adviser. At that time I had kissed three girls, but, after the first, who had splendid Irish, I had found it a rather wearisome occupation. On the other hand, from my considerable reading of French and Russian novels, I felt I had a complete theoretical knowledge of the subject.

'Tell the first girl to go to hell,' I said firmly.

'You cannot do that sort of thing to a girl,' said Phibbs.

'In that case you're going to be pushed into a marriage you don't want,' I said.

'I know that,' he said irritably. 'But I don't know the best thing to do.'

'The best thing is to ask the second girl to marry you at once,' I said.

'Now?' he asked incredulously.

'If you really want to marry the girl, you may as well do it now as any other time,' I said, still rejoicing in my infallibility.

'Oh, of course I want to marry her, but she has to work for a year in London. It seems silly to ask her to marry me just because of another girl.'

'Try her,' I said. 'I doubt if she'll think it's so silly.'

I could usually sound very wise, and I must have done so then, for Phibbs went to London over the week-end, and apparently Norah saw things much as I did. When she returned to Wicklow as his wife I was not so sure of my own wisdom. On the first Sunday when I went to lunch there were no potatoes, and I was scandalized when she went on with her painting and allowed Phibbs and myself to go into town for them. I had never met a girl who forgot things like potatoes, and if I had I should have expected her to repair her omission in silence. I thought Phibbs was too easygoing. Besides, Norah got between him and me in ways I had not anticipated at all. I was as jealous as a schoolboy, and sometimes thought that love and marriage had been greatly exaggerated by the poets and dramatists.

The loneliest creature on God's earth is a young writer trying to find himself, and every few months I took a few days off to stay with the Phibbses, where we talked our heads off into the early hours of the morning about books, pictures, music, religion and sex. I was able to report the arrival at my home in Dublin of the Other Girl's Brother at about seven in the morning. By this time I had bought myself my first dressing-gown and slippers, and when my visitor proceeded to read Phibbs' letters to his sister I was able to strike an attitude and say that I did not wish to listen to my friends' private correspondence. 'But this is about *you*!' he had cried, and went on to read all the witty and malicious things that Phibbs had written of me in the first few weeks of our acquaintance. I thought they were very funny, but managed to remain severe and withdrawn, and the Brother had then set off to drive all day to read to Wilson the references to *him* – not, I hoped, to read the poem on Wilson's wife. In fact, I had liked the Brother and wished I could be more openly sympathetic, because secretly I pined for the days when brothers were brothers and an insult to a woman's honour could only be wiped out in blood.

The Phibbses had rented a little bungalow on a hill over Wicklow town with a garden and a fine view of the sea. Phibbs was happier, more contented, than I had known him, and very proud of Norah – prouder of her than she of him, I sometimes felt resentfully. I was still jealous, and besides I felt he needed a good deal of the sort of admiration that I quite naturally gave him. When we met, there was always an hour or two when he was stiff and perfunctory, but as discussion went to his head the mechanical man dropped away and again he was a creature all fire and air, much as I imagine Shelley to have been.

I had gone after the job in Dublin largely on their account. I planned to have a little flat where they could stay at week-ends, and I could join them in Wicklow. When I left Cork for the last time I took the long train-ride round by Waterford so as to spend a night with them. Phibbs met me at the station and we went up the hill to the bungalow together. He was abstracted and short in speech, but I put it down to the usual awkwardness we felt on meeting again, and I was sure that before the evening was over it would wear off. It wasn't until Norah had gone to bed that Phibbs told me why he was upset. There was Another Man.

Exactly why he chose me for confidant in his love affairs is something I have always wondered about. Ten years later I would have laughed him out of it, but in those years of insecurity light love was as much beyond me as light verse. Naturally, having listened to his iconoclastic conversation for years, I knew in theory that these things happened, and as a student of the nineteenth-century novel I realized that they were more liable to happen in France and Russia than in England – witness Mme Bovary and Mme Karenina – but, so far as my knowledge went, they did not happen in Ireland at all. Sometimes I suspect that this was precisely why he did confide in me, because, 'advanced' as some of his attitudes were, he had others that were not so advanced.

'Oh, I know what you think,' he said bitterly. 'You think I

should have shot them both, and that's how I felt. I walked over the hills like a madman for two days. But that is all only nineteenth-century romanticism. There must be absolute freedom in marriage. That's all.'

'Oh, Geoffrey, you bloody fool!' I said.

I think I began to see then what became clear to me years later, that he was a man who was trapped by his own nature. We are all trapped, of course, sooner or later, but he was more inescapably trapped because in him the gap between instinct and judgment was wider than it is in most of us, and he simply could not jump it. With the two-thirds of him that was air and fire he adopted new attitudes and new ideas, without ever realizing how they contradicted conventions that were fundamental to himself.

Norah was accompanying me to Dublin next morning, on her way to art school in London, and on the train she talked to me about her English friends, each of whom seemed to have Another Man or Another Woman in the background, and I did not wish to say that they all sounded to me as dry as cream crackers. Cream crackers are all very well with morning coffee, but cream crackers for breakfast, lunch and supper as well seemed to me to lack nourishment. So I suffered and sulked the whole way. We went to a party together and said good-bye, she to catch the morning boat to England. By lunch-time I knew she had changed her mind and gone back home, for they both wired me to come down on the evening train. I went round the office singing with sheer relief. The whole thing had been like a nightmare to me.

I suddenly found my whole attitude to Norah changed. Up to this I had been jealous and resentful of her, feeling that she didn't really value the Ariel she had married. Now I saw that she had done what Phibbs could never do, and I could perhaps do, but only after a long struggle, and jumped the gap between instinct and judgment. Women, I think, can do that sort of thing better than men, but not without a considerable amount of self-knowledge and courage. At this point I began to shift my allegiance; for the first time I began to think as much of her as of him.

By evening there was another wire to say that all had been

arranged and that both were leaving for London. I was innocent enough to be glad of that too. But a couple of days later I got a distracted letter from Norah to say Phibbs had gone to live in a flat with two other poets, a man and a woman, both of whom he admired. I also admired the man, but the woman was too modern for my comprehension. To add to the peculiarity of the situation from my point of view, the man had a wife and children who lived on a barge on the Thames.

I could not make head or tail of it. Norah returned, and she, too, seemed to be at a loss. It was part of the cult in this unusual London *ménage* that Phibbs' correspondence with me should be supervised, as in a seminary, and his letters, which had been explosive and malicious, took on a tone of unction more suitable to a hysterical ecclesiastical student. They were sprinkled with words like 'right' and 'wrong', but the moral context was missing. Yeats came back from London with a highly coloured version of the story, and Russell was furious with me for having kept it from him.

This wasn't discretion – nobody has ever accused me of discretion, and that long silence was a strain – but I could not tell it without making it sound like farce, and to me it was not farce, but tragedy, in a language and convention that I did not understand. In my own letters I accused Phibbs of satanic pride and longing for revenge and, though he mocked at me for it, I am sure I was right. He had been hurt, and now he wanted to hurt back beyond the point at which revenge is still feasible and one can hurt without injuring oneself more.

Because I knew he was hurting himself, I decided to intervene. I arrived at the flat that the three poets shared one cold and grey Good Friday. I was shaken when Phibbs told me that the Woman poet was at work and must not be disturbed, because even I was observant enough to see the unfinished sentence in her handwriting on the paper before me, with the ink still wet. I was even more disturbed when I lit a cigarette and he told me that she did not like smoking. She disapproved of ashes – and of crumbs, so we should smoke and eat on the barge. The Woman poet later wrote a novel about it in which I appear as Handy Andy, in love with Norah – Yeats, if I remember rightly, being my rival – but Handy Andy would have been sophisticated compared with me at that Mad Hatter's lunch on the Thames. We drank absinthe and ate salad, and I admired the poet's wife, so when Phibbs walked with me later to the main road I asked in exasperation why, if he was tired of the perfectly good wife he had, he hadn't run away with the poet's wife. I knew nothing of light loves, but I simply could not resist giving my views on them. This, mark you, was the third time I involved myself in Phibbs' love affairs!

I was in a suicidal mood of loneliness as I walked back down the river to London. The public-houses were shut, so I could not even have a drink. There was a pavement artist on the Embankment who, instead of drawing pictures, wrote out little verses, and it was not till I had passed him that I remembered that one of them was the first of the Irish rebel song, 'The Croppy Boy':

> It was early, early in the spring
> The birds did whistle and sweetly sing,
> Changing their notes from tree to tree,
> And the song they sang was 'Old Ireland free'.

I was so homesick that I went back, to give him a shilling and talk to him about Ireland, but I gave up in disgust when I saw that he had changed the last line to 'And the song they sang was "Old England for ever the Land of the Free"'.

I left for Paris that night, and two days later Phibbs bolted after me, but he was so panic-stricken that he immediately set off for Rouen with Norah. They were followed by the two poets and the poet's wife, urging him to return; the hotel manager asked them to leave, and they continued the scene in a cab which drove round and round the town. By this time I was getting bored. Norah and I with our combined puritanisms wanted it to be serious, but it would not stay serious.

And then, to culminate everything, Phibbs went back to London to say he could not go back, and the Woman poet threw herself out of a third-storey window and was visited in hospital by Phibbs and the poet's wife, and Phibbs – always attentive to my good advice – set up house with *her*. In protest against his father's inhuman behaviour in not having invited her beyond the verandah of 'Lisheen', he changed his name by deed poll to Taylor, much in the spirit in which he defaced his books with a rubber stamp. He seemed incapable of withdrawing from a situation when it had became impossible.

After this he taught English for a while in Cairo, but this did not last long either. He found himself at a cocktail party beside a nice man who listened with great interest to his blasphemies and obscenities and asked politely if he was a Communist. 'Good God, no!' said Phibbs. 'I'm an Anarchist.' The nice man did not say, 'And I am the Secretary of State for Education', but he was, and Phibbs had to find himself a job washing dishes in a Cairo hotel. His neighbour and friend in this occupation was the ex-Civil-Hangman of Baghdad, who duly turned up in the batches of poems that reached me.

The poems were not quite so good, and they got decidedly worse after his return to England.

> Changing his notes from tree to tree
> And the song he sang was 'Old England for ever
> the land of the free'.

The atmosphere was too tolerant for his angry, individual humour, or so at least I thought, and he drifted without effort into the attitudes of a mildly eccentric English liberal. As for me, I had made the change to Dublin for no reasonable cause. Dublin without him was empty; there was no writer of my own age to whom I could say the things I said to him, and when I wrote I seemed to be writing only for myself.

9

PHIBBS' defection made the problem of where and how I was going to live worse. There was no longer a bungalow in Wicklow where I could go for week-ends and talk literature, and it seemed pointless for me to rent an apartment, having no one to share it with. Nancy was in Cork, and she was even more evasive on paper than she was in the flesh. Mother was there, and I had more or less determined that I should return there too in a couple of years' time and do what I should have done in the beginning, buy that house that father and I argued about.

I was fortunate in my lodgings, and Mother came on visits and became friendly with my landlady, but I was still dissatisfied. I was rising in the world, but I saw no point in it unless I could have the visible signs of it about me – my own furniture and pictures, my own books and records. I still could not see beyond chattels, and I came some terrible croppers in apartments before I realized that they had to have things like bathrooms, kitchens, light and air, and here Mother could not help me at all because she had as little experience of creature comforts as I had.

I wanted to buy a house for the three of us somewhere on the coast, but Father exploded at the very idea of it. He had agreed to everything else, hadn't he? He had let Mother come and stay with me as long as she pleased. She could go on doing it; he had no objection, but live in a place like Dublin he would not. No more would he come and stay with me for any extended period just to see how he liked it. How could he, with the sort of children that were growing up nowadays, who would wreck his house the moment his back was turned?

It was all true, and I felt guilty about it and sympathized with them in the intolerable separations I inflicted on them; for it would have taken six police to remove Father from his house and more than that to prevent Mother from coming to see that I was all right. Of course, Father was an old soldier and could make himself comfortable in circumstances where another man would perish, but he was even more dependent on her for society than I was. I never had any difficulty in imagining what he felt, having made one of his long pedestrian excursions round the city and filled himself with what for him was hot news – such as how poor Mickie Mac was getting on without the dead sister and what new devilment Gauger in Barrack Street had thought up to plague his respectable daughter-in-law – when he came home to a dark and empty house and had to light the fire and boil the kettle and then read his *Evening Echo* without a soul he could discuss it with.

But I was as helpless against his complacency as he was against my restlessness, and for a month or six weeks at a time Mother would come and stay with me in Dublin, and Minnie Connolly, the saintly old maid at the other side of the Square, would trudge over to listen to Father's news and report to Mother on how he was doing; and when he wasn't 'keeping too good' – her euphemism for going on a drinking bout – Mother would grow fretful because she felt that no one else could understand him or deal with him in that state, and she would go home before her visit was up.

Father and I shared her in the way that men in Phibbs' circle in England were supposed to share some woman while remaining fast friends, but my experience with him had not persuaded me of the possibility of such friendships, and anyhow Father and I were not in the least sophisticated. He was just patiently waiting for some nice girl to marry me and get me out of his hair so that he could have Mother in peace for the rest of his days, while I was hoping by firmness (insisting on my own share of her) and kindness (showing him the considerable advantages of living with me) to wear him down. We were both tolerant, considerate and even generous, but each of us knew that this particular doll belonged to him, and, indeed, it seems to me to say a lot for us that we never really came to blows over her.

At last he agreed to come to Dublin for a few days. He was generous; he did, once started, enjoy free excursions, particularly to a place such as Dublin, where he had been stationed as a young soldier, and he would have a great story for the other old sweats who gathered for Mass on the Sand Quay, but he wanted to make it clear from the start that these would be only excursions and would involve no liability to buy.

He arrived in Dublin with his itinerary in his head. As I remember it, it did not include any tourist monuments and was confined to five military barracks and one cemetery. Each day he set off to perform it on foot, a fine-looking old six-footer with his cap pulled over his eyes, striding along like a boy, interested in every detail. One barrack he visited because he had been stationed there himself, another because my Uncle Tim had been stationed there, a third because some girl he had once tried to pick up in O'Connell Street had said, 'They're a nice lot in the Wellington Barracks', a very ordinary remark which he had trotted out for forty-odd years as though it were a gem of wit. Glasnevin Cemetery he revisited because as a young man he had attended a funeral there and been interested in the graves of the Irish leaders O'Connell and Parnell.

For some reason I decided to go to Glasnevin with him – possibly because he had tried to get there and lost his way. As we came to the Crossguns Bridge he identified the Brian Boru bar with a grin. Obviously he knew it of old. On the way back he stopped outside it.

'You'll have a little drink?' he asked uneasily.

He might well be uneasy, because he knew what I thought of his drinking bouts, and I might have been angry or rude, but there was something wistful about his tone which suggested to me that this might be an occasion.

'Very well, we will,' I said, and we went in and stood at the bar. Father continued to make the pace.

'What will you have?' he asked in a lordly way. 'You'd better have a bottle of stout' – meaning that with a father as broad-minded as himself I need not pretend that I did not drink, and I had the impression that if I refused the stout he would be bitterly hurt.

'Stout will be fine,' I said nervously.

'A stout and a bottle of lemonade, miss,' he said to the barmaid, and then over our drinks he talked to me pleasantly as man to man. Curiously, the conversation has completely left my mind, which shows how disturbed I was, but I fancy he was giving me advice on how to handle Mother – a subject on which, like all husbands, he considered himself an expert. It may have been then that he broke the news to me that Mother was a good deal older than himself and very close to qualifying for the old-age pension.

Being an orphan, she hadn't the slightest idea of when her birthday was or even what her age was. If she was pressed, she would describe her age as 'about sixty', leaving it to mannerly people to say they would never have believed it. But Father was convinced by something my Uncle Tim O'Connor had let drop – no doubt in his well-meaning effort to keep the two of them apart – that Mother was close on seventy and would sacrifice a perfectly good pension of ten shillings a week from mere vanity.

Father, as I have explained, had an absolute mania about pensions. He had wangled two out of the British government, one for long service and another for a non-existent disability. My Uncle Lar, of course, being the smart man he was, had wangled a total disability pension for asthma, which he had always suffered from, and which he could re-energize immediately before a Board by running up Patrick's Hill where the doctors' houses were, but Father always admitted that his brother was a cleverer man than he was. He was looking forward to doing a bit of wangling on the Irish government as well; he would not, of course, get the full ten shillings, but every little helped. It was the nearest thing he knew to an unearned income and the status of a gentleman, and there was much in his attitude to remind me of the retired businessman with his securities. It was not all jam, of course; it had its little tragedies. Lar could get total disability when there was nothing whatever wrong with him, but Father would come back from one of his sessions outside the Sand Quay church, gloomy and disturbed because some old soldier had got total disability, and the other old sweats recognized that he would not be with them for long.

But mainly it was the decency of the British government that he recognized. Here he was, in his sixties, and he could make his daily tours of new building sites and talk patronizingly to the labourers, who would never be able to do the same, but would have to work until they dropped and died in the workhouse. And – as with the retired businessman – there was something ambivalent about Father's friendliness towards the labourers. He was genuinely sorry that they had to go to the workhouse, unlike himself, who could go up to the British Army Hospital in Shanakiel; but he was also proud and pleased that it was they and not he who had to do it.

He had done his best to implant the same sound Conservative principles in Mother, and he simply could not understand that no good-looking woman, however intelligent, wants to be seventy, merely for the sake of ten shillings a week. Now if Father had explained that he only wanted to prove she was fifty, she would have entered into the search with the enthusiasm of a girl, but, as it was, she just listened inattentively to him and continued to look a good ten years younger than himself.

When I tried to pay for the drinks he said nonchalantly 'No, let me do this', and I realized that this, too, was part of the ritual, and probably rehearsed days before. He returned home with me that evening, full of high spirits. He didn't, of course, tell Mother about our little adventure. It was also part of the ritual that you did not tell women what men did when they were out together. It was perfectly easy to rationalize. It was a warm day, and The Boy was thirsty. Ritual is only a linking of the dead with our daily actions, but who among the dead he was trying to impress that afternoon is something I shall never know – his own father, perhaps, or someone he had drunk with there when he himself was The Boy. I only know that I was deeply moved because the little scene had shown me all that had been missing in our relationship and how inspiring it might have been.

It did not, of course, mean that he softened in the least in his objection to living in Dublin with me, or even to staying one day longer that he had bargained for. Sometimes I wonder if he was not afraid that – as with the drink – the first surrender would turn him into an abject old man.

What he felt like at being separated from Mother I could imagine because I had felt it myself, but it never occurred to me that he could feel the same about Cork till one evening when he was staying with us in Glengarriff. For some reason he had been quite reckless and agreed to come for a fortnight, but on the third evening, when he had inspected all the roads out of the little seaside village, I heard him muttering to Mother, half in amusement, half in chagrin:

'My God! Another ten days in this misfortunate hole!'

IO

FOR the first two or three years in Dublin, I organized my library and wrote two books: *Guests of the Nation*, the book of Civil War stories from lodgings in Ranelagh; the novel, *The Saint and Mary Kate*, from my first flat in Anglesea Road, which was neither cheerful nor comfortable, but where at last I had my own books, records, pictures and furniture about me. I still considered myself a poet, and had little notion of how to write a story and none at all of how to write a novel, so they were produced in hysterical fits of enthusiasm, followed by similar fits of despondency, good passages alternating with bad, till I can no longer read them.

All the same, for all its intolerable faults, I knew that *The Saint and Mary Kate* was a work of art, something I had never succeeded in producing before, and as I wrote it, I read it aloud to Mother, who either went into fits of laughter or looked puzzled and said restlessly, 'Well, aren't you a terrible boy!' It became the principal argument of the pious Catholics against me, and at one Library Conference in Cork I had to sit and listen to a denunciation of it as a scandalous and heretical work by the editor of the 'Three Thousand Best Books', who was so drunk that he could not stand straight on the platform.

George Russell enthused about it, not with the enthusiasm of a school teacher whose favourite pupil has passed an examination with honours, but with that of an inhibited man who rejoices in any sort of emotional outpouring – the excitement he displayed over Hugo and Dumas. He was passionately inquisitive about the character of the heroine, and a dozen times at least brought the conversation round to what she would be like to live with. This was something I didn't know myself, because I wasn't really writing about any woman in particular – I didn't know enough of them for that – but about that side of women that appealed to me – the one that has no patience with abstractions. I, of course, was full of abstractions.

Russell was extraordinarily inquisitive about women, and with an ingenuousness that even I found upsetting. Though he never talked to me of his wife, and rarely of the one son he mentioned at all, I had the feeling that he was unhappy in his marriage and inclined to think that women were a plague.

'Do you have flirtations with pretty girls?' he asked me one night.

'Sometimes,' I admitted – I should have hated to confess how rarely.

'And do they get you to write poems for them?'

'Yes.'

'That's fine,' he said happily. 'Write them all the poems they want, but take care they don't marry you. That's the devil of it.'

When he came back from his first American tour he was in a wild state of excitement about American girls. He had spent a birthday in Vassar or some other women's college and the girls had made him a birthday cake with a great mass of candles. Afterwards, one of them had come up and kissed him, and when he started, said, 'Oh, boy, do be your age!'

'They must be the most beautiful girls the world has ever seen,' he said to me. 'If only you could get them to sit in a corner and keep quiet, you could admire them for hours. But they *will* talk!'

At the same time he tried to arrange a marriage between Simone Tery, a beautiful French journalist, and me. He showed his love for Simone as I never knew him to show love for anyone, but knowing his passion for generalization I assumed – quite correctly, I think – that I was not the only young Irish writer he had chosen as a husband for her. He merely adored her, and wanted somebody in Dublin to marry her so that he could be sure of entertainment one evening a week. He got off on the wrong foot with Simone and myself, because when we met for dinner he looked at me and said, 'Isn't she nice?' and then at Simone and said, 'Isn't he nice?' and for the rest of the evening we sat and glowered at one another. He made it worse by congratulating her on not using 'any of those horrible cosmetics that American girls ruin their beauty with', and she, made up as skilfully as only a Frenchwoman can be, modestly lowered her eyes and said, 'I only use them on particular occasions, A.E.'

He was very impressed one night when I repeated a bawdy story a girl had told me and said with great solemnity: 'That is a wonderful example of the economy of Nature which I am always impressing on you. Nature intended me to be a lyric poet, so I *never* met a girl who told stories like that. She intended you to be a realistic novelist, so she just throws girls of that sort in your way.'

I might have said that one reason I did not meet more girls like that was that I saw too much of people like himself. It is the real weakness – if it is a weakness – of the Mother's Boy. It is not that he is not attracted to women, but that he is liable to get into emotional relationships with older men. And Russell suffered as well from a frustrated paternalism towards younger men that was strange in one who had two quite attractive sons of his own. I thought I observed it one night when I got him to talk of the youth of Padraic Colum. Usually he talked in set speeches, which could be very boring, but occasionally, when his memory was jogged by love or hate – or disappointed love, as when Yeats had got beneath his skin again – there was an astonishing change, and you realized that you were dealing not with a pathetic old man, but with a first-rate mind. I had never known him more master of his own cool and sympathetic intelligence than that evening when he sketched for me the picture of an enchanting boy who rushed up to meet you, his overcoat unbuttoned, the pockets of it stuffed with railway waybills and handbills all scribbled over in the intervals of work in the railway offices, and began to read you his latest masterpiece – the great play in which the thud of hoofs continued from first curtain to last – till he suddenly discovered he had the wrong waybills and was really reading from his great epic on St Brendan the Navigator.

I suspected that night that he looked on Colum as his son, and he developed something of the same possessiveness toward me. One night I said something that pleased him and he replied, 'I should have had a son like you, Michael. Don't you think I'd have made a good father for a poet?'

I said something about Diarmuid's being a good substitute, but he laughed it off.

'Oh, Diarmuid has the makings of a very good businessman. Did I tell you I discovered he'd been emptying my waste-paper basket and selling drafts of my poems to an American collector?'

One night a year or two later he called and discovered I had been in bed for a week with bronchitis.

'You should have sent me a wire, you know,' he said with tears in his eyes. 'I'd have come and looked after you. I'm quite a good plain cook, you know. I can cook chops very well.'

Every week he came to my lodgings or flat, on the same evening and at the same hour. Every time he said the same thing, 'My dear fellow, I hope I'm not interrupting you', tossed his coat and hat impatiently on the sofa (once when I took them out to the hall he looked at me slyly and asked, 'Was that necessary?'), combed out his hair and beard, and settled himself in my favourite chair. He was a creature of habit, the sort of man who all his life will sit at the same table of the same restaurant to eat the same meal, and be ill at ease when waited on by a waitress he is not acquainted with.

First, he wanted to know how the writing was going. Usually it was going badly. In those days I wrote in brief excited fits that might be followed by months of idleness and depression, or – what was worse – of fruitless and exhausting labour on some subject I was not mature enough to tackle. A book on Irish literature, which Yeats and he had urged me to write, was not written until thirty-five years later. Sometimes he lectured me on the Dark Fortnight and the Bright Fortnight, one of those generalizations like Leonardo and the Economy of Nature that wore me out. At other times he was really intelligent.

'You know, my dear fellow, a man cannot be so dissatisfied with his own work unless he has much better work to come.'

Once I must really have exasperated him, for he said: 'You know, you remind me of an old hen who has just laid an egg and is going round complaining. Did you ever hear a hen that has laid an egg? She says, "Oh, God! God! God! God! There are going to be no more eggs!" That's what she says, you know.'

He took a cup of tea, clutching the cup and saucer close to his beard, refused a second cup, always in the same dim, hasty way – 'No, thank you, my dear fellow' – while looking at you un-seeingly over his spectacles. Precisely at twenty minutes to eleven he glanced at his watch and gasped, 'I must be going', leaped up as though on wires and fumbled his way downstairs for the last tram. He always stood right in the tracks, signalling frantically with both arms to the driver, and then, without a backward glance, bundled himself on and was half-way up the stairs before the tram re-started. There were no regrets, no backward glances or waves of the hand. His mind was already on something else, like Father's when he was leaving for Cork.

Any break in the habitual round, as when I went home to Cork for the Christmas holidays, irritated him and caused a minor convulsion in his life, and he hit back by complaining that I was 'imperilling my immortal soul by guzzling and swilling'! He was left with a whole evening on his hands that he did not know what to do with, and if he chose to go to someone else's house on that particular evening, there was a reasonable chance that he would continue the practice for the rest of his life, unless they, too, with the incurable instability of human beings, decided to take a holiday or get sick.

For months after I got back I would not see him at all. It was not that he was punishing me for my infidelity, but that he had got himself entangled in some new routine and, since he was com-pletely unaware of it himself, could not get free of it. Then one night I would hear the peremptory, irritable rat-tat-tat that I could tell from hundreds of others, and there he would be tranquilly waiting at the door, stroking his beard, and as he strode impatiently in, without waiting for an invitation, he would say with a sort of happy sigh, 'My dear fellow, I hope I'm not interrupting you.' Another cycle was under way.

He liked fixed days for doing fixed things, and fixed ways of doing them. At one period of his life he painted every Sunday, and the Dublin story was that when he counted his pictures at the end of one year he said in great distress, 'There's something wrong. There are only fifty-one.'

One Monday evening, when the pattern was running smoothly in Mondays, he came in and said without even waiting for an opening: 'I was in Howth yesterday afternoon. I hadn't been there for twelve years. It's very beautiful, you know.'

The face and tone were stoical, but I had the feeling that he was desperately unhappy. I could not imagine why. I have a very slow mind, and it was not until half an hour later that I recognized what it was about the phrase that sounded wrong.

'But isn't Sunday your day for going to Seumas O'Sullivan's, A.E.?'

'Seumas was very rude to Stephens at the Academy dinner on Thursday night,' he said gravely. 'You weren't there. He called Stephens a poetaster. I didn't think that was very nice. I don't think I could ever be friends with Seumas again.'

I was deeply touched by his grief at the loss of an old friend and even more by his loyalty to James Stephens, whom he loved in the almost immoderate way he loved Colum, but I was completely shaken by his next phrase. He gave me a piercing look and asked, 'Michael, has it ever occurred to you that Seumas tipples?'

Literally, there was nothing anyone could reply to that because O'Sullivan's drinking was on the High Court scale. I did not quote Yeat's remark that 'The only trouble about Seamus O'Sullivan is that when he is not drunk he is sober'. I merely felt as I had when Russell had explained that I met girls who told bawdy stories because Nature intended me for a realistic novelist. I could hardly believe that any human being could be so utterly unobservant.

But all ended happily, for the following Monday evening he arrived at my flat at the usual time and – well on in the conversation remarked casually, 'I was at Seumas' yesterday', and I knew that habit as well as old affection had triumphed again.

Russell's old friends loved the creature of habit, the well-tried phrases on the regular evening visit: his enemies detested them. What fascinated me then, and fascinates me still, is the wild creature behind them – the Portadown Presbyterian with his ingenuousness, his loneliness, his unforgettable flashes of genius. And it was hard work to get at it: talk, pictures, poems, everything he did was generalized into insignificance.

Once he asked me to select one of his pictures for my flat, and I chose a painting of a tree by a lake – chose it because it was the only picture in the room that did not contain those dreadful children who appeared in almost every picture he painted and whom he had seen originally in some landscape of Corot's.

'By the way,' I asked, 'what *is* that tree?' I did not mean to be impertinent, but at once I knew I had been.

'Oh, no particular tree,' he replied with a hurt expression. 'Just a tree!'

Everything with him was 'just a tree', not an oak or an elm or an ash; above all, not one with a character or pattern of its own. Habit had obliterated all distinctions.

Even his poems, as often as he repeated them – and he repeated them endlessly – never changed a word or an intonation. He said he knew by heart every line he had written, and this I found hard to understand, because he was the first person to point out to me that language is finite and that its beauty wears away by repetition. But even Yeats' early poems, for all the work Yeats had put in on improving them, never altered by a word or a tone on Russell's lips. He remembered them as they had been written, and though he knew perfectly well when Yeats had improved them, he hated the alterations. If he is the 'old school friend' whom Yeats accused of liking the early poems merely 'because they reminded him of his own youth', that is altogether too simple-minded. Russell was a fine critic, and he knew an improvement the moment he saw it, but the habit-forming complex, like a hardening of the arteries, never allowed him to see Yeats' early work as he saw mine and Higgins' and Kavanagh's, and, though Russell was kind to the point of fatuity, you simply could not take him in. However bad a poet he may have been, he was a poet, and he simply knew.

II

RUSSELL, who was full of Hegelianism, used to argue that Irish literature developed in pairs. There were himself and Yeats, then Stephens and Colum, then Austin Clarke and F. R. Higgins, and now Geoffrey Phibbs and I.

But Russell was an example of another sort of Hegelianism, which he did not observe at all. The rediscovery of Old Irish, on which the whole literary movement was based, had been made by German scholars. When the discovery spread to Ireland the remarkable group of philologists, Irish and German, who worked here was probably the best group of scholars the country had known in modern times, and isolated by their very eminence. When Irish writers such as Yeats and Synge began to make use of the material they unearthed, and wrote as nobody in Ireland had written since the ninth century, they in their turn were isolated, and the two groups were drawn together and existed in an extraordinary love-hate relationship. There were the highly improbable friendships of George Moore and Kuno Meyer, of George Moore and Richard Best, of John Synge and Best. 'Moore didn't know the English language at all,' Best said. 'Moore pointed to a passage in a book and said, 'Best, this man is very ignorant. He writes, "It were better to say". I said, "Moore, that is *not* bad English. That is merely the subjunctive mood." "Best," he said, "what is the subjunctive mood?" I explained it to him, and he said, "But, Best, how wonderful! I shall never again use *anything* but the subjunctive mood." '

Best also explained that Synge didn't know English, but I have forgotten what it was that Synge didn't know. All I do remember is that Synge did not know how to make tea. 'So I said to him,

"Synge," I said, "I will buy you a teapot", and Synge asked, "Best, what *is* a teapot?" ' It would be fascinating to know what other strange discoveries great scholars and writers made about one another.

The truth is that they were friends without knowing why and without understanding the fierce resentments that sometimes blew up between them. They were the nearest thing in nature to the two sexes, for ever scouting about one another's encampments and bringing back horrible tales of what went on in them. Best had the last word on 'that fellow, Joyce', whom everyone talked about. 'He borrowed money from everyone in Dublin, but he never got a penny out of me.'

So it was quite natural that Russell should come to my flat with Osborn Bergin, the greatest of Irish scholars; that we should all meet on Sunday evenings at Russell's and that Russell and I should drop in on Bergin. The only difference was that Russell and I both made tea, but Bergin provided no refreshments. Either he was too much of an ascetic or he was too afraid of his housekeeper.

On the river under the windows of my library at Ballsbridge I used to watch the romance of a swan who had lost his mate and had struck up an immoral relationship with a fussy little duck who was obviously thrilled to death by such a large, strange, beautiful husband. Whenever I watched that strange pair I used to think of Russell and Bergin.

Bergin was a prince of scholars, and the figure I think of whenever I re-read *A Grammarian's Funeral* – who 'gave us the doctrine of the enclitic *De*, Dead from the waist down' – though Bergin wouldn't give you anything, not even a doctrine. 'Bergin's Law', known to all serious philologists, was identified and named by his pupil D. A. Binchy, but Bergin himself never really believed in it. He was a small man with a neat brown beard and a face that varied between the stern and precise and the vague and vacuous. He usually wore a costume that had been fashionable among Irish Nationalists at the time I was born – a tweed jacket, pantaloons and long cycling stockings – and he usually sat with his legs crossed and one eye half closed, making patterns in the air with his pipe. I used to follow the patterns with my eyes, feeling sure that his subconscious mind was writing messages of great significance in the air, if only I could interpret what they meant. Where Russell burbled, Bergin rasped. When he had a story to tell he would pull his legs in under his chair, point at you with his pipe, and screw his face up. When we were alone in his house he would put down his pipe, pick up his old fiddle and play and sing *Gaudeamus Igitur* and other songs from his student days in Germany. His fiddling was worse than his voice, which was terrible.

On one subject he knew more than anybody in the world, and he could not bear to discuss it with more than perhaps five people – rather in the manner of the Lowells and Cabots, and if the God's truth was known he probably thought the Cabots very unreliable. Robin Flower, a really fine scholar, he could not tolerate because Flower spoke Irish with an English accent – forgivable enough in an Englishman, one would have thought.

Nothing would persuade Russell, who knew no language but English, but that I was a formidable scholar too, since I had once, to his own knowledge, caught T. F. O'Rahilly out. O'Rahilly, second only to Bergin in scholarship, though not in crankiness, had a great grudge against Edmund Curtis, the historian, who reviewed books in Irish for Russell's paper, the *Irish Statesman*, and he wrote abusive letters to Russell, suggesting that Curtis couldn't read a page of Irish without a dictionary, till poor Curtis gave up. Russell conscripted me in his place, and in the first review I wrote I came a cropper that wouldn't even have occurred to Curtis, and O'Rahilly wrote his usual letter of complaint, but with what for him was urbanity. He probably felt that if you must have devils you had better have them of your own making. By a coincidence, the very same week that O'Rahilly's letter appeared I got one of his two beautiful anthologies of love poetry for review, and there was a mistake that even a child wouldn't have made. I struggled hard with my conscience, because the book was so beautiful I merely wanted to enthuse and not bother with what to me was nonsense, so I finally ignored it. But I couldn't resist writing to Russell to prove how noble I was, and Russell, walking forth (it was one of his favourite examples of the economy of Nature that he was always talking about), met Bergin, who read my letter with the air of a Lowell being told of a Cabot solecism by a Boston Biddy. 'Nature' must have been working overtime that day because the first person Bergin ran into was O'Rahilly and, in the true Lowell spirit, he showed O'Rahilly the note he had taken. That night, coming on to midnight, O'Rahilly was pounding on Bergin's door, almost in tears, with the cry of 'But I had it right in proof, Bergin! I had it right in proof!' Bergin went round next evening to tell Russell, and Russell wrote to me next morning.

Ah, me! But after that O'Rahilly sent me his works, and was delighted when Thurneysen and I in acknowledging one of them used exactly the same words, Thurneysen in German and I in English. Is it any wonder I enjoyed scouting round the scholars' encampments for what I could bring home in the way of gossip?

But Bergin could not trust a man capable of making a mistake like that. One night, he and I were walking home from Russell's, and I told him I was uncertain of the meaning of one verse in O'Rahilly's second anthology of love poetry. I got a very short answer: 'Couldn't say without seeing the text.' But I was getting used to Bergin's 'Don't knows' and 'Can't imagines' and I produced the book. Bergin took it with great politeness and loathing and stopped under the nearest gaslamp to read. Having read the verse I didn't understand, he turned the page to the beginning of the poem and read it right through. Then he turned back the page and did it again. Finally he closed the book and handed it back to me. 'I'm always telling O'Rahilly not to publish manuscripts he doesn't understand,' he said in a dead voice, and after that he said no more.

He had such a horror of inaccuracy that he avoided the risk of it by never speaking anything but English, except when he was reminiscing, and had it all, as you might say, pat. Once in explaining to me his dislike of the Germans, he described an incident of his student days when he and a French student named Etienne went to register as aliens. 'Osborn Bergin' sounded a good Teutonic name, so he had no trouble, but when it came to the French boy's turn the policeman said flatly, *'Etienne, das ist kein Name.'* According to Bergin, this had given him a hatred of Germans that had lasted throughout his life. When I protested, he said gloomily, 'There are only two tones in the German voice, the whine and the bellow. They're whining now; the bellow will come later.' (This was before Hitler.) I, having no culture at all except what I had picked up from German, protested again, but he crushed me brutally. 'Binchy' (then our Ambassador in Germany) 'says the Germans are a people you keep on trying to like.' That settled that, too. God alone knows what Binchy did say, but this is what Bergin felt he should have said, and it was said on his behalf.

When Bergin and Best went to Germany in later years, Bergin refused to speak German at all, and he let the unfortunate Best struggle with the problem of transport and currency without once opening his mouth. But when Best in Cologne station, having asked Bergin for some small change and got nothing but a scowl, told the railway porter, 'Ich habe nicht Geld', outraged majesty recovered sufficiently to rasp, 'Ich habe KEIN Geld!' Everybody in Ireland knew the story of how when he stood over the grave of his old friend Father Peter O'Leary, he glanced at the breastplate of the coffin and muttered *'Four mistakes!'* but I suspect I was the only person ignorant or innocent enough to challenge him with it. When I did, he merely cocked one eye, made figures on the air with his pipe and muttered 'Well, I didn't make the mistakes, did I?'

He was rather friendlier to the French than to the Germans, and I suspect that if only he could have spoken their language in a way that satisfied his own standards he would have enthused about them. He used to tell with glee a story of Meyer's, who had been with some other scholars at the house of a French philologist and discussed the disappearance of final consonants in the language. The host's old father listened with horror to those blasphemies about his native language, because he knew that final consonants had not disappeared, and at last he whispered in anguish to Meyer, 'Ne le' croye' pa', m'sieu! I' ne sav' pa' ce qu'i' di'.'

And yet, because I loved him, I knew Bergin was a fiercely emotional and possessive man, consumed with obscure abstract hatreds. I know now what I did not realize at the time – what it was that Russell and he had in common. Both were European figures who in their hearts had never ceased to be anything but small-town boys. When Russell was moved he reverted to the Lurgan Orangeman, and when Bergin was moved he reverted to the Cork Gaelic Leaguer. It was an experience to lunch with him and Tadhg O'Donoghue of University College, Cork, who didn't seem to me to have an idea in his good-looking head, though Bergin put on more of a performance for him than he did even for Russell. Bergin had once been Secretary of the Leeside Branch of the Gaelic League in Cork, which had had a disagreement with the Governing Body in Dublin, and when Bergin talked of this disagreement, then forty years old, he became almost incoherent with anger. I never discovered what the Governing Body was supposed to have done, though I listened to the story several times.

Another of his hatreds was George Moore, who, in his usual petulant way, had said to him one night at Best's, 'Oh, Bergin, you bore me!' to which Bergin had retorted, 'I am as much entitled to bore you, Mr Moore, as you are to bore me.' When a man repeats years later the crushing retort he has made, you can be sure that he was badly hurt, and judging by the way Bergin repeated it he must have wanted a writer of his own as badly as Moore wanted a scholar, and felt about Moore's behaviour as a man feels when told by a girl he had been in love with that he was no good as a lover.

His third detestation was Yeats, who, according to Bergin, had insulted him during a meeting of the Dublin Literary Society. 'Dr Bergin, are there any astrological manuscripts in Irish?' Yeats had asked, and Bergin had replied, 'Not to my knowledge, Mr Yeats.' Yeats had then deliberately turned away in his chair. It was no good telling Bergin that Yeats had probably turned away to meditate on the question of whether the British government or the Catholic Church had destroyed the manuscripts. Bergin knew it was an insult intended for him.

But his greatest rancour was reserved for his old friend Joseph O'Neill, a good Celtic scholar, who had been a fellow student of his in Germany. O'Neill – one at least of whose donnish romances will be remembered – married a literary woman, who – again according to Bergin – was always talking of 'Peguy and Proust' and getting the pronunciation wrong – a major offence in anyone but an intimate friend. (When I quoted in German or French Bergin contented himself with following me soundlessly on his lips.)

The O'Neills dropped Bergin, 'a man who couldn't dance either literally or metaphorically', and he resented it fiercely, all the more because Russell replaced him as the O'Neills' best friend, and over the years he made O'Neill the butt of scholarly jokes and poems. The verse squibs began with their student days in Germany and O'Neill's passion for stories of the Wild West:

> *Buffalo Bill war ein Mann*, he read,
> *In des Wortes bester Bedeutung, oh!*

They described O'Neill's days as a school inspector – 'Holy nuns would give him tea, priests would give him dinner' – and described him at his first public function:

> When Gally was young he had more sense
> Than to follow the fiddler and waste his pence.
> Dancing reels on a Galway strand;
> He was saving his feet for a Free State band.
> Heyho, Gallio dancing,
> Slithering, sliding, prancing!
> Heyho, Gallio dancing,
> Dancing at a Free State ball.

And when Russell (who lived round the corner from both

O'Neill and Bergin) reached San Francisco, there was a savage little note waiting for him that read: 'Please remember me to Joseph O'Neill.'

Russell and Bergin were both lonely men, and there was nothing to indicate that one was a widower and the other a bachelor but the fact that the bachelor's house didn't look as though it needed cleaning. Each week they went together to the local cinema, and they carted detective stories to one another's houses. In his days as Editor Russell could glut himself on who-dunits, but now he was often hard up for something to read, and as a librarian I was able to help. Lit up by the discussion of some new gimmick in Agatha Christie or Dorothy Sayers, Russell would expand on the great detective story he would write, called *The Murder of a Celtic Scholar*, with Bergin as principal suspect, though the victim might be Agnes O'Farrelly, Douglas Hyde or even Eoin MacNeill, a fine historian, but 'quite unscrupulous with his sources', according to Bergin. Those were delightful evenings, though when they came to me it took a full week to get rid of the stink of their tobacco. Each year they got someone to drive them into the country, collected masses of coltsfoot, dried it on trays before their windows and then ground it up to mix with their tobacco.

They were always making mystifying little jokes at one another's expense. If it wasn't *The Murder of a Celtic Scholar*, it was Bergin's 'If A.E. had written the Odyssey', a neat little twelve-line lyric in Russell's vaguest manner, which summed up the epic. Then it was Russell writing to Bergin as he crossed the Mississippi, 'which at this point is a mile wide', and Bergin's reply, 'Aristotle says an animal a mile long could not be beautiful, but please don't quote me because I haven't the text before me.' This was reported back to me by Russell with the comment, 'Isn't that just like dear Osborn?'

But in spite of all the joking Russell was very perturbed by the rumour that dear Osborn had written love poetry in Irish which, some friends had told him, was very passionate indeed. I tried to reassure him, but he wasn't satisfied. Russell had wanted a scholar for friend, and if it now turned out that Bergin was really a wild romantic poet whose word no man could rely on, it would be worse than not knowing what to do with his Sunday afternoons. One night he came to my flat, bristling.

'I was at Curran's last night,' he began, without preliminaries, as he did only when he was upset. 'He says Bergin has a poem in all the anthologies which is very passionate. Have you got it? Could you translate it for me? I want to know what it's like.' Of course, I knew it by heart. It was part of the anthology of bad verse I had memorized in the days when I couldn't afford books. It was the plague of Bergin's life, because nobody reprinted it correctly, and it had almost begun to seem that nobody could, as though it had a jinx on it. Bergin had had a circular drawn up, embodying the correct text and demanding a proof.

I translated out of my head for Russell, and after the first few lines he began to stroke his beard and beam like a lover being reassured of his girl's fidelity. 'All literary convention!' he murmured joyously. 'I knew it! I knew our Osborn had never been in love!' (In which, of course, he was wrong, because our Osborn had been very much in love with one of his students; an American girl he had pursued, even abroad; but we cut our friends to suit our needs, and Russell needed a scholar rather than another poet.) So the two elderly men went on happily adoring one another.

Yeats was madly jealous of Russell's scholar and would have given anything to possess one of his own. Nothing would have pleased him better than to be able to say, 'My friend Bergin, the greatest living philologist, tells me...' But, anyway, Bergin wouldn't have told him the time of day. Except among the Lowells and Cabots he never talked of his own subject except to say, 'Don't know', 'Can't tell', or 'Too obscure for me'. He knew I was crazy to learn Old Irish, but the only contribution he ever made to my knowledge of it was when he took Strachan and O'Keeffe's edition of *The Cattle Raid of Cooley* from a shelf one night and murmured, 'Em. Very clean!'

He wasn't at all the dry stick one must make him appear if one is to get the real biscuity Bergin flavour. As with Russell, there was under the urbanized exterior the emotional volcano of the provincial town. Mother adored him, and used to sit at the window, watching for his arrival, so that she could be the first to welcome him. He told her stories of Cork and liked listening to her stories of it. Yeats, of course, either hadn't heard of Cork or didn't think much of it. One night when Bergin was in the flat with us a knock came at the door and she went to answer. A moment later she appeared in the room, looking like a ghost and with her hands in the air. 'Michael!' she cried. 'Yeats!' Then she rushed off to her bedroom, where Yeats couldn't get at her. Yeats, embarrassed by his extraordinary reception, came in looking shyer than ever, and Bergin completed his confusion. Bergin had only to see Yeats to remember that monstrous scene at the Dublin Literary Society.

Yeats and I talked for a few minutes and the name of George Moore came up. Bergin grunted, and Yeats' spirits began to rise, because he began to discern that however much Bergin hated him, he hated Moore worse; and many a dear friendship has begun on nothing more substantial than a common enmity. I could see he was thinking that he might yet acquire a scholar of his own, for he burst into the wonderful series of malicious anecdotes that later appeared in *Dramatis Personae*, along with a number of scabrous ones that haven't appeared anywhere yet.

Bergin was exceedingly vulnerable in his sense of humour, particularly when it concerned a man who had the audacity to say that Bergin bored him. First he chuckled, then he laughed, and finally he was rolling round on the sofa, hysterical with laughter. I had never seen Yeats put on such a performance for anyone before, and I accompanied him to the tramcar in a glow of love and admiration for both of them.

But when I returned, one look at Bergin was enough to dissipate the charm. He was sitting on the sofa, scowling, despising Yeats, despising me for permitting a man like that into the house, but most of all despising himself for the weakness of character that had made him sacrifice his dignity for the sake of a few funny stories. He was already casting himself as Browning's 'Lost Leader' – 'Just for a handful of silver he left us'.

'Isn't he a great old card?' I said as enthusiastically as I could.

'He's a great old cod,' Bergin snapped, without looking at me, and for the rest of the evening I couldn't even get a civil answer out of him.

A scholar's work is often as much a self-portrait as a writer's. Osborn Bergin loved Irish professional poetry of the Late Middle Ages, and to those who knew him the poems give back a reflection of the man. Many of them belong to the Elizabethan period, which was the last great period of Irish love poetry, but it was characteristic of Bergin that he left all that to O'Rahilly. He edited only Cú Chonnacht Ó Cléirigh's *Ní mé bhur n-aithne, a aos gráidh*, and that only because he found it 'mysterious', which it is not, except for the fact that the passion becomes lost in the conceit.

One cannot imagine his friend Kuno Meyer editing them. Meyer was the romantic scholar, and he fell upon the earlier poetry with a freshness and joyousness that can still be felt in his translations, which are all the more remarkable because they are translations from one foreign language into another. According to Bergin, Meyer carried his translations round with him, ready to read to anyone of literary sensitiveness who could produce the perfect word for him. One cannot imagine Bergin doing that. His scholarship was superior to Meyer's and his translations are more exact, but it is the exactness of prose rather than verse. D. A. Binchy tells the story of an English student of Bergin's who once asked in exasperation, 'But what is it all about?' Bergin replied evenly, 'I will give you an exact translation of the words.' And that, too, is characteristic. Even in his choice of words Meyer tries to tell you 'what it is all about'; Bergin gives you the exact prose equivalent and allows you to work out the rest for yourself.

As a result his prose is sometimes more difficult than the verse he is translating. In that beautiful poem on the death of his wife, Muireadhach O'Daly wrote:

Beag an cion do chúl na ngéag
A héag ó a fíor go húr óg.

Bergin translates: 'Little was the fault (or affection) of the branching tresses that she should die and leave her husband while fresh and young.' But whether *cion* means 'fault' or 'affection' it would be more polite to translate: 'It was no blame to the girl of the branching tresses' or maybe even 'It was small desire the girl of the branching tresses had to die'.

It was not that Bergin was insensitive to what the Irish said. On the contrary, he merely believed, as he said himself, that they were as untranslatable as an ode of Horace. When I took him up on this, and translated 'A Winter Campaign' into the pseudo-Horatian metre of Marvell, he ignored both the compliment and the criticism, and I gathered I had committed *lèse-majesté*. He was touchy about any slighting remark regarding the poems themselves. Once, when I had mentioned them in the same breath with the verbose eighteenth-century poets, he replied stiffly, 'Those men were aristocrats and scholars.' He liked the aristocratic flavour, but even more he loved the neatness, the order, the scholarship and the feeling of an Oxford common-room.

That strongly donnish note existed in Irish poetry from the beginning, but in these poems it is at its strongest because the world they knew was collapsing in ruin about its authors. I think Bergin liked to remember that even in the days when earth was falling, 'the day when earth's foundations fled', these Irish professional poets continued to count their syllables, and admitted no word, no grammatical form, which their masters of two hundred years before would not have approved. Like other artists, he identified himself with his subject, for he was one of the last of a great generation of scholars in a country where scholarship was no longer regarded.

12

WHAT Yeats had come to see me about was his Academy of Letters, which still drags out some sort of shadowy, precarious existence. The idea of it was sound enough – a solid body of informed opinion that might encourage young writers and discourage the Catholic Church from suppressing them; but for both purposes it suffered from the fact that, apart from Yeats, its most important members lived in England and had no notion of what conditions in Ireland were like.

The Dublin committee was Yeats, Russell, Higgins, Robinson, O'Sullivan, Gogarty and myself, 'two of whom', as Yeats said in his oracular way, 'make themselves drunk and a third who came drunk from his mother's womb'. The two who made themselves drunk were O'Sullivan and Robinson, and, as he explained to me later, Yeats had to invite Robinson to tea before every committee meeting in order to supervise his drinking and make sure he reached the meeting in a sober state. The one who came drunk from his mother's womb was Oliver Gogarty, 'the kindest heart in Dublin and the dirtiest tongue', as a friend of his described him. I knew the kindness. I had been only a short time in Dublin before a surgeon ordered me into hospital for an operation on my throat. A friend of mine told Gogarty, and he said, 'Tell him to come round at once.' I went, and Gogarty, who did not know me at all, began by apologizing for the creator of the universe in a way that endeared him to me. 'You know you're in the cancer group,' he said gently, and then spent ten minutes looking at my throat. 'Jesus Christ!' I heard him muttering. 'There are doctors in this town that don't know the difference between cancer and a sore toe.' After that, he sprang into rambunctious life. 'There's nothing wrong with you, only Indian tea. I'll write it out for you – you can get it at Roberts' – Lapsang-Soo-Chong. I'm like Yeats; "I have forgotten all my Hebrew." ' I couldn't help liking Gogarty, though he did make a vicious attack on me later at an Academy dinner, describing me as 'a country boy with hair in his nose and hair in his ears and a brief-case in his hand'.

However, Yeats was a natural organizer, never happy unless he was organizing something or somebody – a great bully, as I discovered later, and an outrageous flatterer. When I, who at the time had not even produced a book, questioned the inclusion of St John Ervine in the Academy, Yeats did not say, as he should have said, that Shaw insisted; he merely asked mellowly, 'Why worry about literary eminence? You and I will provide that.'

When he began to bully me I always gave him lip, almost on principle. After my father, I never quarrelled so much with anyone, and even if one allows that I am a bit in the same line myself, it takes two to make a disagreement last as long as ours. One might say that I was discovering my real father at last, and that all the old attitudes induced by my human father came on top. Yet I can truthfully say that when, towards the end of his life, I became his devoted slave, it was entirely due to his generosity, because with no one else was I so crude and uppish.

His principal weakness was that he was easily bored, and L. A. G. Strong was not the only one who bored him. George Russell bored him too, and many others, and he made no effort to conceal it. This, I think, cost him the affection of a number of people who would have been better friends than some of those he made.

Apart from these things, I think of him as a shy and rather lonely man who desperately wanted to be friends, and was utterly loyal to the friends he made. It took a long time to appreciate that shyness in him because it tended to make him portentous and overwhelming in society and even in the home. Once, when Michael Yeats was pulling his sister's hair and Mrs Yeats failed to separate them, Daddy was summoned. He stalked slowly and solemnly to an armchair, sat down and recited, 'Let dogs delight to bark and bite', and then stalked out again, apparently feeling he had done all that was expected of a father. The children never became intimate with him: even the marvellous 'Prayer for my Daughter' was written while Anne was safely in another building. Michael once got his own back by asking in a piercing voice as his father went by, 'Mummy, who is that man?' and Yeats was deeply hurt.

Mrs Yeats was my favourite among authors' wives. This was an old romance, dating from my earliest days in Dublin, when again and again she had covered up my shyness and awkwardness. One evening someone had lured me to a fashionable party at Gogarty's. I was sitting on the floor wishing I was dead when the door opened and George Yeats came in. She gave one look round the room and then came and sat beside me.

'How did you know the way I was feeling?' I asked.

'You looked exactly as Willie does when he gets shy,' she said with a grin. 'You were running your hand through your hair.'

I used to think no one in the world suspected my attachment, least of all George Yeats, though nowadays I wonder if Yeats himself did not suspect it.

The only person I ever heard him speak of with real malice was George Moore, and that still puzzles me a little, because he was a remarkably tolerant man. I have a suspicion that it was because Moore had hurt Lady Gregory by describing herself and her family as 'soupers'. You could say anything you liked about himself, or even his family, but his toleration never really extended to people whom he thought had injured either Lady Gregory or Synge. He was generous enough in his public references to Arthur Griffith, but there is submerged ice in that line that describes 'Arthur Griffith staring in hysterical pride', and Padraic Colum once said to me, 'Yeats never had any time for me after *The Playboy* row.' More than anything else that happened to him I suspect the quarrel about Synge's great play really hurt him.

We had our first big show-down at an early meeting of that wretched Academy when Yeats demanded that Russell, the

Secretary, should change the minutes of the previous meeting. Yeats had apparently said something he should not have said and wanted it omitted. As a public official I knew that the minutes were perfectly correct, and since everybody else was afraid to oppose Yeats I said so. As a friend of Russell's I also knew that he was terribly hurt, and when Yeats persisted in his rigmarole I flew at him.

The minutes remained as they were, and when everyone else had gone home I stayed to comfort Russell, who was close to tears.

'Yeats has always been like that,' he said bitterly. 'Always unscrupulous and always dishonest.'

Naturally I believed him, without wondering why on earth he had let me defend him instead of standing up for himself. It was only later, when I got to know both men better, that I noticed more and more in Russell the oscillation between love and hatred of Yeats. It worked both ways, of course. Yeats was intolerable with Russell, and one of my most shameful evenings was when I joined Yeats in baiting him; but, on the other hand, Russell was never so dull with anyone as he was with Yeats, who, when he became embarrassed, could be outrageous. Russell complained to me that, when cornered in an argument, Yeats would wave his hand and say loftily, 'Yes, Russell, but that was before the peacock screamed' or some other bit of nonsense. This was exactly what Yeats was likely to do when he was bored, but, on the other hand, Russell did bore him. He even bored me occasionally.

Once, when I arrived at Russell's house in Rathgar before he was ready to receive me, I noticed the proofs of *Song and its Fountains* on his desk with a dedication to Yeats, 'Rival and Friend'. (The dedication has since been printed in a different form, but I think I am right about the one I saw.) The revealing phrase was deleted from the printed book. Russell was not only too modest a man, but too good a critic not to know that there could be no rivalry between himself and Yeats, and somewhere in him there was a sense of failure that came out in his evenings with

Yeats. Behind it all, I think, was Yeats' resentment at Russell's not having taken Synge's side in the *Playboy* controversy and letting his house be used as a headquarters by the anti-Synge faction, but this was all so long before my time that I could not have been sure of identifying it. What I am sure of is that Russell needed Yeats' pity, and Yeats had no pity. He could give you things that I think now were more worth while – admiration, tolerance and absolute loyalty, but he was as pitiless with others as he was with himself.

By this I do not mean that Russell was his inferior, if such judgments have any meaning. He was one of those people, like Desmond McCarthy, whom I later became friendly with, who love writers and books for their own sweet sake, have no apparent jealousy, and who, though first-rate men themselves, will appear hardly at all in literary history.

A week or so after the quarrel I have described, Russell resigned from the secretaryship of the Academy, giving as his reason that he 'would have nothing more to do with us or with a country so given over to the devil', as Yeats quoted him in a letter to me. The quotation is probably correct because, as I shall have to explain, during his last year in Dublin Russell was exceedingly depressed. Yeats thought he was just afraid of a row.

'Russell is always timid before a row begins,' he wrote to me, 'though when it does he fights like a madman.'

This was true enough, but I suspected that it was not Russell's real reason, and I told Yeats he had been insufferably rude. He took this reproof from a young and unknown writer with extraordinary graciousness. 'I must smooth him down,' he said mildly, washing his hands with an episcopal air.

He had been reading a novel by Austin Clarke, one of the young writers Russell felt he had discovered, and reading it with genuine admiration, but instead of writing to Clarke as he would normally have done, he wrote to Russell, congratulating him on being the first to appreciate Clarke's gifts. 'As usual, you were right and I was wrong,' he wrote.

Russell, who was always pathetically grateful for any little tribute from Yeats, rushed round to my house to show me the letter. 'I think that's very noble of him, don't you?' he asked ingenuously, and, pleased to see him happy, I agreed. Of course he wrote at once to Yeats, withdrawing his resignation, and things went on as before. I could not resist making fun of Yeats about it, and told him I was writing a book of stories in which all my acquaintances would appear in the historic circumstances that suited them best, and that he was being described as a Renaissance cardinal. He chuckled, because he loved to be thought a really smooth intriguer, which he wasn't. 'Ah, we know one another so long,' he said modestly.

The Irish Government had just banned Shaw's *Black Girl in Search of God* as being 'in its general tendency indecent and obscene'. It was a crude effort of the Censorship Board to prevent the teaching of Rationalism, and the one small peg they had to hang the charge of obscenity on was the woodcuts of a naked girl. There was no clause in the Act which permitted the Minister to ban any pictures, even if they were obscene, and I wanted to use the book to fight the Censorship Board. I argued that if Shaw, Yeats and lesser writers like myself took the Abbey Theatre for one Sunday in the month, lectured and sold copies of the book, we could force the government to withdraw the ban because even Mr de Valera's government would hardly be idiotic enough to prosecute Shaw and Yeats, but Yeats felt he was too old and ill to face a public campaign, so we compromised on a deputation to the Minister of Justice, Patrick Rutledge.

It seemed to me important that we should not offer Rutledge the excuse of having banned the book on account of the pictures, because only if we could get him to state this himself could we show that the order was illegal. Accordingly the deputation – Yeats, Russell, Higgins and I – agreed that we should confine ourselves to the text and make no mention of the pictures unless the Minister mentioned them himself.

But next morning when I arrived at Government Buildings, there was Yeats with a suspicious-looking folio under his arm. 'What is that?' I asked, and, with the air of a small boy caught at the jam, he said angrily, 'These are reproductions of the frescoes by Michelangelo in the Pope's private chapel.' I said that we might as well go home, but it was no use. Yeats had made up a beautiful speech on the Sanctity of the Nude and he intended to deliver it to somebody.

He did, and Russell added a few useful observations about Victorians who put trousers on table-legs, while I fumed and Higgins chuckled. As an old trade-union official he knew as I did exactly how much the Sanctity of the Nude troubled the sleep of an Irish politician. That night in the foyer of the Abbey Theatre the Minister grabbed Higgins by the arm and said, 'Yeats thinks I'm going to use what he said about the dirty pictures in the Pope's chapel. What a fool I am!'

All the same, Yeats refused to quarrel with me. He published two books of my translations from the Irish and re-wrote them in the process. Gogarty once invited me to come to Yeats' flat with him – 'He's writing a few little lyrics for me, and I'd like to see how he's getting on.' It *was* rather like that. I went one night to Yeats' for dinner and we fought for God knows how long over a single line of an O'Rahilly translation I had done – 'Has made me travel to seek you, Valentine Brown.' At first I was fascinated by the way he kept trying it out, changing pitch and intonation. 'Has made me – no! Has made me travel to seek you – No, that's wrong, HAS MADE ME TRAVEL TO SEEK YOU, VALENTINE BROWN – no!'

Long before that evening I had tired of the line, and hearing it repeated endlessly in Yeats' monotone I felt it sounded worse.

'It's tautological,' I complained. 'It should be something like "Has made me a beggar before you, Valentine Brown," ' and he glared at me as if he had never seen me before.

'No beggars! No beggars!' he roared, and I realized that, like other theatre men I have known, he thought the writer's place was at home.

All the same, it was as interesting to work over poetry with him as it was later to work over plays. He was an absolute master of both, and his principal virtue was his principal defect. He had absolutely no ear for music that I could discern, though this, of course, never shook his faith in his own musical genius. He told a story of how he had gone to Dr Sigerson's one day when Sigerson had an old countrywoman in a hypnotic trance and made her feel Yeats' face. 'Poet', she had said, then 'great poet', then 'musician'. 'And then I knew she was a genuine medium,' Yeats declared.

He was pleased when someone said he had a 'natural' ear, and, for all I know, this may have been true: he certainly had not a cultivated one. When I returned from a holiday in Italy and told him of the folk-singing I had heard on the canals in Venice, he asked me modestly if it was anything like his own. Nevertheless, it saved him from the sort of jingle that poets with too sensitive a musical ear fall into, and the harder he worked at writing words for music, the more unmusical they became. Even when he revised the O'Rahilly translations I had done, which were in alexandrines, he treated them as though they were in iambic pentameter, unaware that he had dropped a beat.

His musical adviser was F. R. Higgins, another old friend of Russell, and up to a short time before Yeats' death his most intimate friend in Ireland. For years the one fathead wrote what he thought were songs, the other fathead fitted them, as he believed, to old Irish airs, and they got a third fathead to take down their nonsense in staff notation. If Russell and Bergin were a queer pair, Yeats and Higgins were queerer still. Higgins was huge, fat and handsome, with a red face and black, lank hair that tumbled in a lovelock over one eye and tiny feet that would not support his Falstaffian frame. He was emotional, indiscreet and generous, and, after talking to him for an evening, you were left with the impression that you had made a friend for life. But he left you, and within ten minutes was giving himself with equal generosity to your worst enemy and, before even he knew what he was doing, was betraying you all over the shop.

I once said of him that he was a Protestant with all the vices of a Catholic, but *because* he was a Protestant, and had set up a little trade journal of his own and lived off the small proceeds, and had bought himself a little bungalow on the Dodder, and was a kind and considerate husband, he kept building up in himself an enormous feeling of guilt, so that when you next met him he was merely wondering how much you had heard of his witty description of you and what plots you had thought up to get your own back on him, till at last you felt he was no friend at all, much less a friend for life.

Once, after a meeting of Yeats' moribund Academy, when O'Faolain and myself had been trying to get Ernie O'Malley elected, we had a drink with Higgins and then went out to Yeats' house. Yeats greeted us with his Renaissance cardinal's chuckle and asked: 'What do you two young rascals mean by trying to fill my Academy with gunmen?'

We realized at once that Higgins had been on the telephone to report everything we had said in the most disparaging way, and I said in exasperation, 'Trust you to make a friend of a man who is uneducated, intellectually and emotionally!' Yeats gave a great guffaw, but, as always happened when he felt he had been rebuked, he must have brooded on it, because he replied to it a year or so later.

'You don't understand my friendship with Higgins, O'Connor, but when you reach my age you will find there is one thing a man cannot do without, and that is another man to talk to him about women.' To someone else he said, 'X comes here and talks to me about women, and it is all invention. Higgins comes sweating from his whore and every word rings true.' But there was much more to his friendship with Higgins than that. It was characteristic of Yeats to deprecate the genuine warmth of his own attachments. He needed Gogarty and Higgins as he needed the women he talked to them about, because they broke through the barriers he could not help erecting about himself.

Higgins never knew when he had been rebuked. Yeats felt he had been rebuked even when – as on that occasion – no rebuke had been intended.

But God help Yeats if he really listened to Higgins' romances! At regular intervals he fell in love as we all do, always madly and for the first and last time, and Dublin resounded with his confidences distributed generously like everything else he had and always under a vow of secrecy; and when his unhappy passion reached its inevitable tragic conclusion he fell ill, always with cancer or something equally incurable. He knew that no ordinary doctor would be heartless enough to break the news to him, but he knew how to beat that too. He applied for a life insurance policy, had himself examined by the insurance company's doctor, and when the policy was accepted tore up the papers and rushed into town to drink with his cronies.

Unfortunately, it was to Higgins that Yeats found it easy to confide all his little domestic difficulties. It was typical of Yeats' capacity to size a man up that with me, on the contrary, his references to sex were usually almost boyishly modest and even made me impatient. He knew, too, though I never told him so, that I did not share his interest in spiritualism. One night I asked him bluntly if he ever had had an experience that could not be explained in strictly rational terms. He thought for a while and grew embarrassed.

'Yes, once. I think I can tell you. You are, after all, a man of the world. I was having a love affair with a certain woman and she said she was pregnant. I was very worried because I felt that if she was, I must marry her. I came home to Ireland and confessed to an old aunt. "Don't believe her," she said. "She's having you on." So I went to a certain famous medium and asked for her help without telling her what my trouble was. She went into a trance and produced some writing that neither of us could read. Finally I took it to the British Museum and they told me to come back in a week. When I went back the head of one of the departments said, "Mr Yeats, this is a most remarkable document. It is written in the form of Hebrew taught in the German universities in the seventeenth century."'

Then Yeats looked at me triumphantly, his head tossed back, the big, blind eyes behind the spectacles challenging me to explain that one if I could.

'Never mind what sort of Hebrew it was written in,' I said.

'Did it tell you whether you were the father of the child or not?'

The practical Corkman! He sat back wearily – rationalists are so hard to argue with.

'Oh, no, no,' he said vaguely. 'It just said things like "O great poet of our race!" ' Clearly he thought this important, but I didn't. As a storyteller I felt that the point had got lost.

'Well, there wasn't any necessity for saying that in Hebrew,' I said, and this too, like the business of Higgins, rankled because I got the usual well-thought-out retort a couple of years later.

What Yeats did not know was that his harmless little crushes on younger women and every small disagreement in the home would be repeated by Higgins within an hour in an exaggerated and witty way in some Dublin public-house. This embarrassed me, not because I am not indiscreet myself and don't enjoy gossip like the next man, but because Higgins' gossip had an element of intrigue in it. It was almost as though by telling you funny stories about your friends he was ingratiating himself with you and lining you up against them. Gogarty's gossip, which was much more slanderous and a breach of professional confidence besides, since Yeats was his patient, was so disinterested that it seemed to get lost in its own malice, and you could laugh at it without feeling that you were betraying anybody or anything. To stop him in a story would be like stealing a bottle from a baby, but it was almost like doing a kindness to Higgins.

Once when he was telling some story about the Yeatses that embarrassed me, I got up in a hurry and said, 'And yet I never leave that house without feeling like a million dollars' – a queer phrase for me to use, and one that shows how uncomfortable I felt. But the effect on Higgins was even stranger. There were tears in his eyes – tears of real affection – and he replied, 'And I feel exactly the same.'

Of course he did, but he simply could not resist a good story when it aligned you against someone who was involved in his intrigue – innocent intrigues enough, God knows, because he was fantastically generous. There was the occasion, for instance, when Yeats was reported to be dying in Majorca. I can still remember the lights flashing it out over O'Connell Bridge and feeling sick at heart. Robinson and Higgins, in a state of maudlin emotion, arranged for the lying in state in the foyer of the Abbey Theatre with a wreath of laurel over Yeats' head – 'not *plain* laurel, Fred,' Robinson sobbed, 'but the small-leafed poet's laurel.' When Yeats recovered and came home, this was much too good a story for Higgins to keep from him – since it showed Robinson in a ridiculous light. It never once crossed Higgins' mind that an old and sickly man might not appreciate the comedy of his own death.

'You needn't go on,' growled Yeats. 'It reminds me of my two uncles, one of whom was drunk and the other mad, quarrelling over my grandfather's open grave as to which of them was to inherit grandfather's musical box.'

Yeats' comment was so much better than the original story that Higgins had to come and tell me about it, and I don't think that even then it occurred to him that it contained a rebuke. Which, of course, was also what was nice about Higgins, even when he did not know that he was being nice.

In his last phase, when I knew him, Yeats was by way of being a Fascist, and a supporter of O'Duffy. He wrote unsingable Fascist songs to the tunes of 'O'Donnell Abu' and 'The Heather Glen' and caused me acute embarrassment by appearing at dinner in the Kildare Street Club in a blue shirt. At the same time there never was anyone with less of the fanatic in him. He took a mischievous delight in devilling anyone who took politics too seriously. One evening in the Club he insisted on introducing me to an old Unionist, and then, when I'd left, made the old man's life a misery by telling him that I was a notorious gunman and a supporter of de Valera. He told of a London party where a duke had come up to him and said, 'I suppose you support Dr Cosgrave?' 'Oh, I support the gunmen – on both sides,' said Yeats. 'And what did he say?' I asked. 'Oh, the damn fool turned his back on me and walked away,' Yeats said in disgust.

I had to threaten to resign before I got him to drop the proposal to produce *Coriolanus* in coloured shirts at the Abbey, and even after that he deliberately provoked me by coming out to dinner with me again in a brilliant blue shirt. Mrs Yeats, who was English, was a strong supporter of de Valera and hated all Fascists, including her next-door neighbours, who were Blueshirts also. Now Mrs Yeats kept hens and the Blueshirts kept a dog, and the dog worried Mrs Yeats' hens. One day Mrs Yeats' favourite hen disappeared, and she, according to W. B., said, 'It's that damn Blueshirts' dog', so she wrote a very stiff letter to the neighbours accusing the dog of having made away with her hen. 'But you see, O'Connor, the neighbours are Blueshirts, with a proper sense of order and discipline, and within an hour or two back comes the reply, "Dear Madam, Dog Destroyed." Now, George is English, and like all English people she has a great tenderness towards animals, and I left her almost in tears for the death of the Blueshirt dog.'

The second part of the story came a few nights later when Yeats said to me, 'O'Connor, you remember the story I told you about the Blueshirt dog and the democratic hen? The democratic hen has come back. George is overwhelmed with guilt. She wants to write an apology to the neighbours, but I say to her, "It is too late for apologies. No apology is going to bring the Blueshirt dog back to life."'

Both the Yeatses are in that little story; the sincere and sometimes cranky public man, and the tolerant and affectionate husband and friend who, like the plain girl at the party, does not miss a single move.

13

By 1932 I had begun to notice that Russell was becoming more and more emotional. This was the year of his wife's death, and he could not manage the unnecessarily large house with just the aid of an old housekeeper.

I was unwell, and my doctor, Richard Hayes, ordered me away for six weeks, so I took a seaside house in Glengarriff for myself and Mother. Father came down for a fortnight, but it nearly broke his heart.

The Eucharistic Congress was being held in Dublin, and during the preparations Russell got himself involved in a newspaper controversy with a Jesuit whom he slaughtered. The Jesuit complained to me about his conduct. 'There were three courses open to Mr Russell: he could have denied my major, denied my minor, or said that my conclusion did not follow. What did Mr Russell do? He ignored my syllogism entirely. That is not the conduct of a gentleman.'

Russell came to spend the week of the Congress with me, and Osborn Bergin accompanied him. On the way down he was interviewed by a reporter from the *Cork Examiner* and not only denounced the Eucharistic Congress, but recited in full Oisin's great tirade against St Patrick. Bergin discovered a mistake in the recitation, but he told me admiringly that he could not have believed in such a perfect verbal memory. After having let off all that steam Russell was in high spirits and his conversation was full of mischief and invention. While Bergin and I swam, he sat on a rock, sketching and commenting to the Celtic gods on the thunder that rolled promisingly in the distance.

'Oh, come on, come on, Mananan! You can do better than

that. All I want you to do is to wash out those damned Christian idolaters.'

Bergin's swimming was like his scholarship. He could only do the breaststroke, but he did it perfectly and effortlessly, and when I attempted the crawl he trod water and glared at me, even without glasses. 'What's all the splashing about?' he asked.

I rowed them to Bryce's island, where Russell had stayed as a young man. 'I gather I should encourage you with a boat song,' he said. 'As I can't sing, I'll recite instead.' And he did. His high spirits were dimmed when Mrs Bryce took us to a corner of the island and said, 'Don't you remember this, A.E.? This is where you saw the vision.'

'There are places like that, you know,' he said curtly to me, but I saw that he was glad to escape from her and suspected that he was just a little tired of elderly ladies reminding him of the mystical experiences of his youth, particularly when he had managed to forget all about them himself.

Each day as we went walking we found a young painter stationed in the roadway with his easel, painting like mad and pretending that he did not know who Russell was, until Bergin and I flatly told Russell he would have to talk to the young man. He was genuinely shocked. He may have seen the vision, but he did not see the painter. Next day he went straight up to the easel and gave his views with his usual frankness and kindness.

'Young man, I think you've been painting in a rather dry climate?'

'Yes, sir. I've just come from Spain.'

'Well, this isn't Spain, you know. This is a very damp climate. Between us and those mountains there are half a dozen planes of moisture. Those are what gives it its luminousness.'

After supper the three of us went up the hill to the field where the young painter was camping out, and as Russell squatted happily on a rock to look at his pictures a country girl rose, like an apparition against the sky, above a loose stone wall with something large clapped to her backside.

'Well, Nellie?' the young painter said, and she held up a portrait of herself as though dissociating herself entirely from it.

'Dey say 'tis AWFUL!' she said.

The poor young painter was getting a bad time that night, for as we left I heard Bergin chuckling happily to himself.

'What's that?' I said.

'Twenty-two per cent,' said Bergin.*

Next evening another painter – a much more famous one – dropped into the hotel to see Russell, and he was in a state of intense misery. He had studied Glengarriff closely, and except for one old wooden pier by the hotel there was nothing at all to paint.

'Nothing?' Russell said delightedly. 'All those mountains and woods and water?'

'Nothing,' said the painter. 'It is all too saturated with the essence of what it is.'

It was a delightful holiday, but it was the last flash of the gay and youthful Russell. He was becoming more and more angry and afraid before the new Establishment of priests and politicians, particularly Sean MacEntee and de Valera. One night he really frightened me by cursing de Valera in the way I had seen old women in Cork curse – raising his arms above his head and giving himself up entirely to his emotion.

'I curse that man as generations of Irishmen to come will curse him – the man who destroyed our country!'

One night that winter he came to my flat, bewildered and distraught. He told me that he had just received a warning that he had only a short time to live. I knew he did not mean that he had seen a doctor: he was much too plain-spoken to conceal a fact like that, and besides, when his illness really became a subject for doctors he was the first to accept their optimistic prognosis.

'I wasn't told how soon,' he said. 'I dare say it could be a month or a year.' He was not afraid of death, but he was afraid of the pain and humiliation that would precede it – 'the immortal soul being kicked out of the world like an old sick dog with a canister tied to his tail'.

I did my best to comfort him, but I was not very successful,

* Bergin's judgments, based on his own set of criteria, were frequently expressed in percentages.

partly, I suppose, because I did not really believe in his premonition, but largely because I had little or nothing of the genuine religious feeling of himself and Yeats. It was not for lack of good will. I knew that their search for religious truth, no matter what absurdities it had led them into, had given them an intellectual richness that I had not got; I had let them argue with me and had read the books Russell lent me, but it hadn't affected my own way of thinking in the slightest.

'Why do you shut your eyes to those things, O'Connor?' Yeats stormed at me once when I told him the story of an old priest in Ballingeary who was supposed to have been shot by the Queen of the Fairies. 'You know perfectly well that things like that were once the religion of the whole world.' On another occasion, when I had to tell Russell that I had got nothing from a reading of Mme Blavatsky, he replied angrily, 'Oh, you needn't tell me! Like all Irish Catholics you are just an atheist at heart.'

That night, after we had discussed his premonition of death, Russell and I talked of the immortality of the soul, and he gradually began to brighten up.

'Socrates is the fellow I want to meet,' he said, laughing. 'I have lots of questions to ask him about some of the things Plato makes him say. Who do you want to meet? Tolstoy, I suppose?'

'No!' I said. 'Certainly not Tolstoy.'

'I couldn't stand Tolstoy either. I don't mind being told about my faults by people who like me, but Tolstoy didn't like anybody.'

And curiously, when he left and I accompanied him home, he was in the highest of spirits again. He had talked himself happy.

But a week or two later I was seeing him home again and quoted a poem I had just written which began:

> A patriot frenzy enduring too long
>   Can hang like a stone on the heart of a man,
> And I have made Ireland too much of my song;
>   I will now bid those foolish old dreams to begone.

He stopped dead at the corner of Appian Way and threw his arms in the air in a frenzy.

'That's exactly how I feel,' he cried. 'I have to get out of this country before it drives me mad.'

Soon afterwards he told me that he had made up his mind to give up his Dublin house and take a flat in London. He also talked of going on a world cruise and visiting his son Diarmuid, who had married in America.

Yeats was puzzled and, as always when there was something that he did not understand, inclined to mockery.

'Indian saints give up the world when they reach a certain age,' he said to me. 'Russell is a saint, but he is also a great journalist, so he's giving up the world to go on a world cruise.'

Nothing could have been wider of the mark. Of all the men I have known, Russell was most a creature of habit, and for him to give up everything – his house, his books, his pictures, his friends – was already a sort of death. Unless, indeed, it is that these were the death he wished to escape from, the inextricable patterns of habit that encompassed his fiery soul. Whatever it was against which he had erected them had breached them at last. I would have done anything to comfort him, but how can you comfort a man who does not weep, who perhaps himself does not know what it is he wants to weep about?

He asked me to come to his house the week before his departure and take whatever I wanted of his things, but I could not endure the thought of taking things that had been dear to him, and I did not go.

Then one evening Higgins came to my flat with peremptory instructions from Russell to bring me along with him. Higgins himself was close to tears, and I had never liked him so much as I did that evening.

'You'll have to come,' he said. 'A.E. will be hurt if you don't come, and the man is hurt enough.'

'How can I go to the house of a man who's hurt like that and take his things away?' I asked.

'How do you think I did it?' Higgins asked. 'I've had to sit there and listen while they said, "Oh, A.E., I wonder if you could let me have that nice little drawing by So-and-So?" You should see the greed in those fellows' eyes.'

I went back with him. Russell's face was like a tragic mask as he showed other friends about the rooms and let them take his little treasures. By this time I was as emotional as Higgins, and the longing to weep only made me angry. I told Russell that I did not want to take anything of his, and he said in a broken voice, 'You mustn't leave without taking something. I put aside a set of the Jack Yeats' broadsheets for you. I know you admire Jack Yeats. Do please take them.'

I stayed on and Higgins stayed with me and we made casual conversation as we might have done at a wake, only that on this occasion the corpse made one of the company. When we left, the pubs were shut. Otherwise I think we would have got blind drunk.

Russell left for London, and for the first few months our friendship remained as close as ever. As anyone might have predicted, London was a disappointment to him.

'It is really a dead country,' he wrote to me, 'but there are very nice people among the dead, and if they were only alive they would be the best people in the world.'

He wrote to me that he was unwell and that his London doctor had diagnosed colitis. That evening, when I was walking on Sandymount Strand with my own doctor, Richard Hayes, I showed him the letter.

'I am very sorry to say that is not colitis,' he said after a moment. 'That is cancer.'

I did not take this any more seriously than I had taken Russell's own premonitions, but I was deeply upset by certain caustic remarks Higgins reported him as having made, and our friendship cooled off. It was only long after, when I got to know Higgins better, that I wondered whether those unpleasant remarks had ever been made outside the excitable, devious imagination of Higgins himself, because that Till Eulenspiegel of a man delighted in nothing so much as embroiling mutual friends and then grieving uproariously over the sufferings of both.

When Russell died, he grieved louder than ever, because Yeats refused to speak over the grave. 'If I spoke I should have had to tell all the truth' is the excuse Higgins reported his making, but what that meant I do not know – unless, perhaps, Higgins had made mischief between Russell and Yeats as well. I made the speech, and Yeats stood behind me, an old man who looked as though he had not long to live himself, and opposite me, at the other side of the grave, was de Valera (in those days it was not considered a sin for a Catholic to attend a Protestant funeral). When I had finished, Yeats in his generous way stepped forward and took my hand, saying in a loud voice so as to be heard by everybody, 'Very fine! Very noble!' and then, in a whisper, 'Have you copies for the Press?'

Of course I hadn't, which is probably as well because in those days I could be both pompous and silly. What I should say now is, 'This was the man who was father to three generations of Irish poets, and there is nothing more to be said.'

Later, when I told Yeats how strange it was to speak about Russell, with all his enemies round the grave, he grumbled, 'I know. I saw them too. I'll beat them yet, though. I've arranged to be buried in Sligo where nobody but my friends will follow me.'

Poor man! That was all he knew.

14

RICHARD Hayes, the man who had spotted what was wrong with Russell, was the local dispensary doctor. I had gone to him in the ordinary way as a patient, and we had become friends. He was a tall, thin man with a melancholy face, a big nose and a prominent chin that made you think of a punchinello. In the evenings he called for me and we went for walks along Sandymount Strand, dropping into his house on Guilford Road on the way back for a cup of coffee or a drink. Years before, in the internment camp, I had noticed how uninquisitive and unrevealing men friends can be, and it was only after I had known him for some time that I realized that he was one of the heroes of the 1916 Rebellion and had been sentenced to death by the British. His brother, a delightful old priest from County Limerick to whom he introduced me, had also distinguished himself by defying some British general. As Irish people put things, the Hayeses were a 'decent' family.

I discovered it only by accident and by what later seemed dramatic irony. One evening when he was coming to my flat I invited James Montgomery, the film censor, and his wife. Montgomery was one of the greatest of the Dublin wits, and, though I had no great liking for wit and detested the Dublin brand, I was very attached to Montgomery. He was a natty little man with a red face and a Roman nose and an extraordinary sweetness of character, as though he had been steeped for a decade in a vat of port wine. He is the man I think of in the part of Mr Bennet in *Pride and Prejudice*, and a prig like Darcy might account him a failure, because his talent, which was cynical, was at war with his temperament, which was humble and given to hero-worship.

Like Mr Bennet, Montgomery had his domestic troubles, for he was married for the second time to a great beauty, much younger than himself, and their verbal tussles were part of the Dublin legend. She indulged in palmistry, and that night she read Hayes' palm and said, 'There's some terrible crisis here. It's as though you'd died, and then started to live again.' Hayes was slightly shaken and left early, and Montgomery said excitedly to me, 'You realized what the crisis was, didn't you? He was sentenced to death and then reprieved. Ethel hasn't a notion who he is.'

A day or two later Hayes said to me, 'You didn't know the crisis Mrs Montgomery was referring to. It was true enough. I was only once in love, and then it was with a girl who had tuberculosis. I was a doctor, and I knew how long she had to live. I couldn't bear the thought that my children might be the same way, so I gave her up.'

Hayes' main interest was the Irish on the Continent in the seventeenth and eighteenth centuries. He had admirable manners; a trifle too elegant – even pompous – but no more disconcerting than those of the few French aristocrats I have met. I felt sure that the poor people of Ringsend adored him, because, though he stormed and screamed at them when they got him out of bed or interrupted him late at night when he was reading, he always went to them, always on foot.

His scenes with them were also very French. 'What are you saying? Why don't you speak up, man? How do you expect me to hear you? I asked what your name was ... Murphy? Never heard of you, my good man. Your wife is poorly? I don't know your wife, and I don't know you. How long has your wife been "poorly"?'

'Well, she was took bad this morning, doctor.'

'She was took bad this morning! And you wait until midnight to drag me out of my house in the pouring rain! What sort of conduct is that?'

'Well, doctor, I only got in myself at half six.'

'Oh, so you got in at half six. Your day's work is over at six o'clock and nobody can disturb you. But when will I get in? You make me sick! Where did you say you live?'

They knew he got into such tizzies, and if the truth was known probably enjoyed them as much as I enjoyed the other sort of tizzies he got into. He would fly into sudden, old-maidish fits of self-righteousness when he felt that the memory of some famous Irishman was being slighted. O'Faolain and Frank MacDermott, working on the manuscript of the Wolfe Tone autobiography, had discovered a passage that Tone's son had omitted which showed that Tone, the great lover, had had a mistress, and Hayes pleaded with me to persuade O'Faolain not to publish it. I laughed so hard that he complained of me to a group of his old political associates at Sean MacEntee's, and they laughed even louder.

'You may laugh,' he said pompously to me, standing up before the fireplace. 'But you remember what Goethe said – "The Irish are always like a pack of mongrels dragging down some noble stag."'

'You got that quotation from Yeats, Dick.'

'Never mind where I got it. It's true!'

'And neither you nor Yeats ever read a word of Goethe in your lives. If you had, you'd know that the "noble stag" was the Duke of Wellington and the mongrels were O'Connell and his party.'

'Oh, what rubbish!' he snorted, all his indignation diverted for the time being onto Goethe.

I enjoyed those evening strolls with him because he raised his hat and bowed very low to every poor slum woman he knew, and saluted every man, and sometimes would stop to introduce them and make them show off. He bent his long frame in two like a jack-knife, his walking stick thrust out from behind his back like a tail and his punchinello face distorted with amiability, and said in that angular way of his, 'Oh, Jim, I wonder if you would mind telling my friend that shocking experience of yours with the Black and Tans – you remember, that night they threw you into the river? I often wonder how you survived it.'

He even brought me with him on his visits to the slums and introduced me as a young doctor, inviting my opinion on certain marks and symptoms, but after the first time I refused to go. I thought it might be dangerous for himself and felt it was humiliating to patients. As a doctor he did not see it in that light at all. He liked them, and he gave them better service than they would have had from most doctors they would have had to pay.

I am not observant, and for a long time it did not strike me as strange that this distinguished man should be in such a modest job, for even at medicine, which he usually merely made fun of, he struck me as brilliant: I have described how he had diagnosed Russell's disease from a few lines in a letter. It took me even longer to realize that, far from having been slighted, Hayes had refused every sinecure he had been offered. It was when we argued about this that I came across the other side of the man – the side that did not ring altogether true – a mock modesty that amounted to arrogance.

Then one day the British and Irish Press were full of the story that he was to be made Governor-General – representative of the British king in Ireland. I thought he would be an admirable choice. That night, after he had dodged the reporters, we went for our walk as usual and argued all the way. He protested rhetorically and insincerely that it was not a position for someone like himself, an obscure dispensary doctor with an amateur's interest in history. Suddenly the humour of it seemed to strike him and he stopped and laughed loudly and heartily.

'You needn't tell me what you really think, O'Donovan,' he said. (He called me O'Donovan only when he wanted to mark the distance between us.) 'I can see the very thought in your mind.'

'What's that?' I asked.

'I'll tell you,' he replied, bending double and thrusting his jaw forward with a glitter of daft humour in his eyes. 'You're thinking that never before in your life have you had to deal with a man of such insane vanity.'

Almost literally this had been what I was thinking, and my protest did not come quick enough.

'I knew it,' he said with a crow of triumph. 'And you're right, of course. I am mad with vanity.'

For several years he was my dearest friend, the man who replaced Corkery in my affections, to whom I went in every difficulty and who gave me advice that was always disinterested and sometimes noble. This, of course, was not all clear gain. This dependence on older men was part of the price one had to pay for being a Mother's Boy. It was not he who suggested that I should write a play about the Irish Invincibles or a biography of Michael Collins, but I doubt if without him I should have written either. That might have been small loss, but without him I should have had no help from any of Collins' friends. Some had not even helped Beasley,* who was himself one of Collins' associates, but they were prepared to do anything for Hayes. It was the first time I realized the extent of his influence.

We had one extraordinary experience while I was writing the book. The hardest man in Ireland to get at was Joe O'Reilly, Collins' personal servant, his messenger boy, his nurse, and nobody – literally nobody – knew what O'Reilly could tell if he chose, or could even guess why he did not tell it. He was then Aide-de-Camp to the Governor-General; a handsome, brightly spoken, golf-playing man who could have posed anywhere for the picture of the All-American Male.

Hayes' invitation brought him to the house in Guilford Road one evening, and for a couple of hours I had the experience that every biographer knows and dreads. Here was this attractive, friendly, handsome man, completely master of himself, apparently ready to tell everything, but in reality determined on telling nothing.

Hayes was puzzled – after all, he was a historian – and he took over the questioning himself. He was a much more skilful questioner than I, but he too got nowhere.

And then, suddenly, when I was ready to give up and go home, O'Reilly collapsed – if the word even suggests what really happened, which was more like a building caving in. Something had gone wrong with him. Either he had drunk too much, which I thought unlikely because he was perfectly lucid, or, accidentally, either Hayes or I had hypnotized him.

* General Piaras Béaslaí wrote the first biography of Collins, *Michael Collins and the Making of Ireland* (Dublin and London, 1930).

I can remember distinctly the question that precipitated his collapse. I had asked, 'How did Collins behave when he had to have someone shot?' and O'Reilly began his reply carefully, even helpfully, in such a way that it could be of no possible use to me. Then he suddenly jumped up, thrust his hands in his trousers pockets and began to stamp about the room, digging his heels in with a savagery that almost shook the house. Finally he threw himself onto a sofa, picked up a newspaper, which he pretended to read, tossed it aside after a few moments and said in a coarse country voice, 'Jesus Christ Almighty, how often have I to tell ye . . . ?' It was no longer Joe O'Reilly who was in the room. It was Michael Collins, and for close on two hours I had an experience that must be every biographer's dream, of watching someone I had never known as though he were still alive. Every gesture, every intonation was imprinted on O'Reilly's brain as if on tape.

I had seen that auto-hypnotism only once before. That was in 1932 when Mother and I were travelling by bus from Bantry. One of the passengers was a violent, cynical, one-legged man who began to beg, and the conductor was too afraid to interfere with him. I took an intense loathing to him and refused to give him money, but he was much less interested in me than in some members of a pipers' band who were also travelling. He demanded that they should play for him, and when they merely looked out of the windows he began to imitate the bagpipes himself. After a time I realized that the bagpipes he was imitating were those he had heard during some battle in France fifteen years before. The bagpipes hypnotized him, and now he began imitating the sound of a German scouting plane, the big guns, the whistle of the shells, and as they fell silent he began to mutter in a low frenzied voice to someone who was beside him. 'Hey, Jim! Give us a clip there, Jim! They're coming! Hurry! Jim, Jim!' He reached over to shake someone and then started and sighed. Then he took an ammunition belt that was not there from the shoulders of someone who was long dead and slung it over his own, fitted a clip – that gesture I knew so well – into the heavy stick he carried and began to fire over the back of the seat. Suddenly he sprang into the air and fell in the centre of the bus, unconscious it seemed, and for some reason we were all too embarrassed to do anything. After a few minutes he groaned and reached out to touch his leg – the one that wasn't there. Then he got to his feet and sat back in his seat perfectly silent. I have rarely been so ashamed of myself as I was that day.

But the scene with O'Reilly was almost worse because you could see not only Collins, but also the effect he was having upon a gentle, sensitive boy, and it made you want to intervene between a boy who was no longer there and a ghost. I did it even at the risk of breaking the record. He was sobbing when he described how Collins had crucified him till he decided to leave. 'Here!' was all Collins replied. 'Take this letter on your way.'

'But didn't anybody tell him to lay off you?' I asked angrily.

'Yes, the girl next door,' he said. She said, 'Collins, do you know what you're doing to that boy?' And Mick said (and suddenly Collins was back in the room again), 'I know his value better than you do. He goes to Mass for me every morning. Jesus Christ, do you think I don't know what he's worth to me?'

When O'Reilly left, the handsome, sprightly young man had disappeared. In his place was an elderly, bewildered man, and you could see what he would be like if Collins had lived. Hayes detained me, and as he refilled my glass he asked, 'Have you ever seen anything so extraordinary?' We both doubted if O'Reilly would turn up next evening.

He did; but this time he looked like the ghost. He gave me a pathetic, accusing look.

'I don't know what you did to me last night,' he muttered. 'I couldn't sleep. I never did anything like that before. I can't stop. It's going on in my head the whole time. I have to talk about it.'

He did so for the rest of the evening, and once again Collins was there. Nowadays a tape recorder in the next room would probably catch most of it, but I had no way of getting it down because I did not dare take out a notebook.

The sequel to that was interesting too, for when the book on

Collins was published O'Reilly was reputed to be going through Dublin like a madman, threatening to shoot me. One day, he and I met in the middle of Grafton Street. There was no escaping him and I stopped. 'I've been trying to see you,' he muttered. 'Come in here for a cup of tea.' I went along with him, wondering what I had started, but all he wanted was to tell me the book had already gone out of print and he wanted a half-dozen copies to send to friends. Reality, I suppose, is like that. One looks at it and turns away, appalled by the Gorgon's head. And then one realizes that one has lived with it, that one has no other reality than the fact that one has once looked at it with naked eyes and survived.

Some years previously Hayes had published a couple of books on the Irish in France, which had had a sort of local success, but had scarcely paid for the cost of their production. He was now writing a book on the French Invasion of Ireland. I accompanied him on some of his trips in search of material. Again, his wide influence worked wonderfully. Seán McKeon led us to one old man whose grandfather had told him the story of the invasion. It was an extraordinary experience because the old man was a character out of Thomas Hardy, a mere vehicle. He pronounced the name of the French general, Hoche, in the French way, and then added apologetically, 'That's how grandfather used to say it, Oche.'

Although I had done some work on that book, there was no reason for my name to appear in it at all. Yet in the final draft, Hayes intended to print a few lines of a '98 song which I had translated for his amusement. But after an interview with his publisher he came to my flat while my mother was staying with me. Everything else the publishers would stand – but not my name on the title-page. According to Hayes' version of the interview, I had mistranslated the lines, misinterpreted the sentiments.

The lines, for all the little importance they have, were:

> The sturdy Frenchman, with ships in order,
>   Beneath sharp masts is long at sea;
> They're always saying they will come to Ireland
>   And they will set the poor Irish free.

Rather than sacrifice the book, he had sacrificed the lines, and I had heartily agreed with him. At that time, rather than see that book unpublished, I would have eaten everything I had ever written. But years later this event was sharply brought back to my mind when Dick Hayes himself was the author of an attempt to censor my writings.

15

THE other friend of those years in Dublin was the curate in the Star of the Sea church in Sandymount, Tim Traynor. I had met him first through Sean O'Faolain when he was curate in Adam and Eve's church. He brought us down to the vaults to see the coffin of Leonard MacNally, the informer who betrayed Robert Emmett, and as we left he gave the coffin a thundering kick. He did the same with all visitors, and it was something you liked or did not like as the case might be. It was so typical of Traynor that I liked it.

We became friends only when he came as curate to Sandymount and lived in the presbytery in Leahy's Terrace – beautifully described by Joyce. It was almost the fashion to say that he was an interesting man who should never have been a priest, and Hayes – the seed and breed of priests and himself everything I admired in certain priests of the older generation – said it to me several times. I knew he was warning me against Traynor, and if he had seen me at a country race-meeting, putting on bets for Traynor, who was not allowed to bet himself, he would have said it even louder. They disapproved of one another, and Traynor in his conspiratorial way told me that Hayes owned slum property.

He had the sort of face that I now see oftener in New York and Boston than in Ireland – the pugilistic Irish face, beefy and red and scowling, with features that seemed to have withdrawn into it to guard it from blows; a broad, blunted nose and a square jaw. Except for the good looks, it had a lot in common with the face of Fred Higgins, as his character had a lot in common with Higgins', for when I described Higgins as a Protestant with all the vices of a Catholic I might, but for the one small difference, have been describing Traynor. He was as conspiratorial as Higgins and much more malicious. If you were injured by one of Higgins' intrigues there was nothing much to blame for it but the will of God, but Traynor, in pursuing some imaginary grievance, would invent and carry through cruel practical jokes. When he swaggered into my room of an evening I would sometimes ask, 'Well, which is it to be tonight, Nero, Napoleon or St Francis of Assisi?' Most often it was Nero.

'It's that fellow Jenkins. Wait till I tell you!'

Yet I never really felt that he was not a good priest, and he gave me an understanding of and sympathy with the Irish priesthood which even the antics of its silliest members have not been able to affect. It was merely that his temperament and imagination constantly overflowed the necessary limits of his vocation as they would have overflowed the limits of almost any calling, short of that of a pirate. Yet they also enriched his character, so that you felt if he lived for another twenty years he would be a very fine priest indeed. It was significant to me that our old friend, the Tailor of Gougane Barra, who had a trick of nicknaming all his acquaintances in ways that stuck instantly, christened Hayes 'The Old Child' and Traynor 'The Saint'. There *was* an element of childishness in Hayes, and you always underestimated Traynor if you paid attention only to the devil and forgot the saint.

It was characteristic of him that he became really friendly with me only when he discovered that as boys we had both had a romantic crush on the same girl. He had had better fortune than I, for one night he had seen Natalie home from college up Summer Hill, and all the way they had held hands without exchanging a word. When the man she was proposing to marry had held back, she had complained of him to Traynor; he had advised her and they had remained friends until her death.

It was also characteristic of him that when I left his rooms that night he insisted on my taking the only picture he had of her. That was not only the new friend and the outburst of generosity; it was also the priest who knew he should not brood on a dead girl's picture.

But, of course, he brooded just the same. The emotional expansiveness that overflowed the limitations of his profession made him brood on all the might-have-beens of his life, and they were endless. I used to make fun of his rooms, which were a museum of all the might-have-beens: books on science, history, art; paintings, sculptures, a shot-gun that needed cleaning and a cinematograph that wouldn't work – all passions pursued with fury for a few weeks till each in turn joined the exhibits on view. It was not only Nero and St Francis who alternated in his strange, complex character, but Einstein, Michelangelo and Gibbon as well.

Sometimes, when I visited him, he would come to meet me with the big fist out, swaggering with excitement.

'How are you? You're looking fine. You'll have a drink. Listen! I have a great wine here. This is something special.' (Just like a boy with a new gadget.)

'How much did it cost, Tim?'

'Five and six,' he would say wonderingly, turning back from the drink cupboard. 'He had only a case of it left. Wasn't I lucky? Wait till you try it!'

Wine was only a sketch of an escape route, because Traynor was no drinker. Another, and more profitable one, was a career in the world. One evening, when he came to me, acutely depressed about some frustration, I asked, 'Tim, why the hell don't you cut your hook and get out?'

Traynor had no intention of cutting his hook, and he knew me too well to imagine that I was slighting his vocation; it was the chance of exploring another might-have-been that attracted him.

'Why?' he asked shamefastly. 'What could I do if I did get out?'

'You wouldn't starve.'

'Maybe I wouldn't, but what could I do?'

'If you'd gone to America five years ago you'd probably be a millionaire by now.'

'Do you think so?' (By this time he was beginning to light up again.)

'I'm damn sure of it. I can easily see you in a big office, giving everyone hell.'

'You might be right,' he admitted wistfully. 'I'd love to be able to get things done.'

He was always trying to get things done, and he wasn't always as successful as he was with St Brigid's thighbone. This was a marvellous story, and all the more remarkable because he did not realize how funny it was. He was curate of a new church in Killester which was being dedicated to St Brigid, and in one of his manic phases Traynor imagined how wonderful it would be if the church contained a genuine relic of the saint. The only reported relic was a thighbone, which was in a convent somewhere in the Peninsula – Portugal, I think, or it may have been Spain. He got round his parish priest – parish priests are the bane of an active curate's life – received the blessing of the kindly old archbishop, Byrne, and set off armed with letters of introduction to the Portuguese Department of Antiquities, the Portuguese Foreign Office, and above all to the Cardinal who controlled the contents of churches, monasteries and convents throughout the country.

The trouble was he could not get anywhere near the Cardinal.

Day after day he haunted the Cardinal's palace, and the greasy Monsignore who acted as his secretary said regretfully that the Cardinal was away, that he was opening a convent outside the city, was at lunch with some gentleman from the Curia, or was merely taking his siesta and could not be disturbed. Meanwhile Traynor's leave of absence had almost expired, and he dreaded the thought of returning to Dublin without having accomplished anything whatever.

'I was desperate, I tell you,' he said, scowling with remembered panic. 'That last day I went up I saw the same greasy brute. No, the Cardinal was lying down. No, immediately he got up he would have to leave for an important engagement. So I said to myself, "There's nothing those dagoes can do to me. I'm not in my own diocese." And I just took out my wallet and handed the Monsignore a pound note. "For your charities, Monsignore," I said, and he glanced back over his shoulder and said, "Wait a moment, Father. I think I hear His Eminence's footstep. Perhaps he hasn't retired yet. Do come in."

'He showed me into a bloody enormous waiting-room with folding doors, and he left me there for about five minutes. Suddenly the folding doors were thrown back and in came this wizened-looking old woman of a man and sat down in a big chair. I knelt and kissed his ring, and then I told him what I came for. He put on a sad air.

' "But you see, Father," he said, "this convent is in a very remote area. The people are poor; they are rather simple-minded and they have a great veneration for St Brigid. I am afraid, Father, that if there was any question of interfering with the relic there would be danger of violence. In my position I cannot risk the possibility of riots and publicity. I am sure you will understand." "I understand, Your Eminence," says I.

'And then the same idea crossed my mind and I nearly laughed into the old ruffian's face. "I'm not in my own diocese. There's nothing whatever he can do to me." So I put my hand in my pocket and took out my wallet – did you ever see a film called *The Clutching Hand?*'

'No.'

'Well, you should. Because it happened to me. Suddenly I saw the Clutching Hand reaching out for my wallet – like a bird's claw with the long nails on it. Before I could take it out he had the five-pound note out of my fingers. "One moment, Father, and I'll see what I can do," he said and left the room. In another ten minutes back comes the greasy Monsignore with the written authority for me to break the thighbone of St Brigid and bring it back to Ireland with me.'

And then, because he was proud of his Church, he gave me a dirty look and said, 'You can say what you like about the Irish priests, but you couldn't buy an Irish bishop for five pounds.'

But, of course, marriage was the greatest might-have-been of all, and on that he could talk for hours. Like most priests (and indeed lawyers and doctors), he had seen its shady side. When my own marriage (which he had opposed) broke up, he stopped all traffic at a busy intersection to come out of his car and shout at me, 'I *told* you she was too tough for you!' Even Natalie's marriage he felt bitter about because she had talked too freely of the man she had married; and when he was telling me about some particularly sordid episode he had encountered in his parish, he comforted himself with the usual seminary sour grapes. Once he told me about a parishioner who was convinced that his wife was trying to poison him, and another night about a man and wife who occupied separate rooms and communicated only by notes in the hallway.

'There's marriage for you now!' he said with gloomy pride.

'Oh, for God's sake, that isn't marriage,' I replied.

'It could have happened exactly the same to me,' he said.

'It couldn't,' I said. 'It could happen only to someone who had the capacity for behaving like that. You haven't.'

'What do you think I'd have done?' he asked, delighted to explore imaginatively that land which for him would forever be unknown.

'Nothing, probably,' I said. 'You'd have been too busy, worrying about the kids.'

'You might be right there,' he said scowling. 'I often wonder what sort of father I'd have made.'

'You needn't worry,' I said. 'You'd have been a very good one, only a little bit too conscientious. You'd have fretted yourself into the grave about their marks at school.'

'That was the way Mother was with us,' he said.

He had a peculiarly intense relationship with his mother, who, after his father's death, had brought up and educated two fine sons entirely by her own efforts as a dressmaker and small shopkeeper. He was too clever not to have observed all her little foibles and vanities. He had been compelled to wear an Eton collar, which distinguished him from the toughs of the neighbourhood, and he had not quite forgiven her that. She had had him trained to play the violin, and a neighbouring shopkeeper with a son who was to be a priest had taken up the challenge and had her son taught to play the piano. As the other shop had a narrow stairway the piano had to be lifted by crane to an upper-storey window, which had caused the Traynors great satisfaction.

But when he had to play at a convent concert and the rival shopkeeper had arranged that his name would be omitted from the concert programme, she had stalked out of the concert hall with Traynor at her heels and refused to allow him to play at all. ('And you were perfectly right, Mrs Traynor', her friend among the nuns had told her.)

'Once, when I was at University College, Cork,' he said to me, 'I made an excuse not to come home for the week-end. I pretended I had a lot of work to do, but, really, all I wanted was to get off with a couple of fellows for a week-end in Youghal. When we were walking along the promenade, who do you think we met, but Mother? She'd got lonely at home and come down for a day excursion. When she saw me she smiled and bowed and said, "Good evening", and all I could do was to raise my hat. But after that she wouldn't even let me talk about it. "Ah, you have no word!" she said. Wasn't that a terrible thing for her to say – "You have no word"?'

It was a phrase my mother used to me. 'Word' meant 'honour', and I knew exactly how he felt.

At the same time he was too imaginative a man not to realize the full extent of her sacrifice for himself and his brother. When she died, he felt it was his duty to read the Burial Service.

'Don't do it, Tim,' another priest warned him. 'You'll only break down.'

But Traynor felt he owed this last duty to his mother. He didn't even need to read the service: he loved the poetry so much that he knew it by heart and recited it to me, but the poetry was too much. After a few moments he burst into helpless sobbing, and his friend took the book from his hand and finished it for him.

All the imaginative improvisation was only the outward expression of a terrible inward loneliness, loneliness that was accentuated by his calling. In that sense only could I ever admit that he was not a good priest – he should have had a tougher hide. Priests in Ireland are cut off from ordinary intercourse in a way that seems unknown in other countries. Once when we were arguing he made me impatient and I said, 'Ah, don't be a bloody fool, Tim!' His face suddenly went mad, and for a moment I thought he meant to strike me. Then he recollected himself and said darkly, 'Do you know that nobody has called me a bloody fool since I was sixteen?' Then the humour of it struck him, and he described how, once, when he was home on holidays from the seminary he was pontificating at the supper table and suddenly caught his uncle winking at his mother. Then he grew angry again.

'People like you give the impression that it's our fault if the country is priest-ridden. We know it's priest-ridden, but what can we do about it? I can't even get on a tram without some old man or woman getting up to offer me his seat. I can't go into a living-room without knowing that all ordinary conversation stops, and when it starts again it's going to be intended for my ears. That's not a natural life. A man can't be sane and not be called a bloody fool now and again.'

That, of course, was my function, though we both knew that his friendship with me was highly dangerous to him. One night after dark, when he was sitting with the other two curates on the sea-front, I passed and he hailed me. Immediately the others rose and strode off without an apology, while Traynor sat there, mad with chagrin, muttering, 'Dirty ignorant louts!'

Before I knew him he spent his holidays as a stretcher-bearer in Lourdes: somehow the contact with people who were ill and dying satisfied the gentleness and protectiveness in his nature. There was an enormous amount of this, but it never went on for long because when he felt rebuffed, brooding and anger took its place. In those years he took every chance of spending a few days in Gougane Barra in the mountains of West Cork. He stayed at the inn, abandoned his Roman collar and served at the bar, went fishing and argued with the visitors and (if I knew him) got involved personally and vindictively in every minor disagreement for miles round. His loneliness was of a sort that made it difficult for him to become involved with anything except as a protagonist. Most of his evenings he spent with Tim Buckley, the Tailor, who had nicknamed him 'The Saint'.

The Tailor was a very remarkable man, a crippled old man of natural genius, with a wife as remarkable as himself. Ansty was thin, tragic and sour; the Tailor was plump, wise and sweet-tempered. He sat on a butter-box and blew the fire with his old hat, and carried on an unending dialogue with his wife about the fire, the cow and the Cronins who kept the inn, but their real subject was always human life. He was one of the greatest talkers I have known; and if in the way of great talkers he did occasionally hold the floor too much, it was never because he was self-assertive, but because he had a sort of natural authority that asserted itself without assistance. He suffered from the fact that his cultural tradition was an oral, and hence a very fallible one, so that faced with the unfamiliar it always rationalized, turning everything to folklore. For instance, nothing could persuade him but that the Boer general, De Wet – one of the heroes of his youth – was not a County Cork man who had introduced himself to the black men with a 'Dia dhuit', the Gaelic 'Good day', and much of what he took for granted was of the same order of knowledge. But he knew almost all that was good in the oral tradition, and because he was a man of natural genius was never completely contained in it, and like Traynor himself he overflowed.

Literally he was a man who did not know which century he lived in. He lived it intensely in his own as perceived from a little cottage above the mountain road to Gougane Barra, with Hitler, St Patrick and Danny Cohalan, the Bishop of Cork, as strict contemporaries. His favourite song in English was 'The Herring', which Cecil Sharp collected also in the Appalachians, but any story or verse he quoted might be of the nineteenth or the fifteenth century, or indeed, from the world of prehistory, and he used it all to serve his own Johnsonian purpose of commenting on the vagaries of human existence. When Ansty tried to rouse him to a state of activity which he found unnatural, he blew the fire with his hat and commented on her folly in the words of the Gárlach Coileánach – 'My mother was drowned a year ago; she'd have been round the lake since then'; and it was only after his death that it dawned on me that the Gárlach Coileánach was only a corruption of Gárlach Ioldánach, the Youth of Many Arts, which is one of the ancient names for the Celtic god Lug who gave his name to such faraway places as Lyon and Laon. 'Take life easy and life will take you easy,' he used to say, and life had taken him fairly easy up to that: he had never seen a volcano or a bishop in eruption. His time was coming.

I spent one delightful Christmas with Traynor in Gougane, because I knew that he was feeling restless and lonely. There was no one else at the inn but a middle-aged lady who had known Sir Basil Zaharoff intimately from childhood and had come to spend a few days of perfect peace in the mountains. Traynor, who was gloomily convinced that she was having us on or someone was having her on, had her luggage examined and it contained two dance frocks that Ansty made great play of. 'Jesus Christ!' she would mutter mournfully, returning from one of her excursions after the cow. 'Two young strong men and no wan at all to give the poor woman a tickle!'

The Tailor knew that I was searching for a song called 'Driving the Geese at Evening', which was too broad for the local folklorists to record, and he had ordered down old Batty Kit from the hill to sing it for me. At the sight of Traynor Batty dried up; it was not only in the towns that the conversation changed when a priest came into the room, but the Tailor would have none of this. ' 'Tis a bit barbarous,' Batty said. 'Even so, even so,' said the Tailor. 'It wasn't you who wrote or composed it.' Actually, Batty was crazy to sing. He was a melomaniac and in spite of his great age had a beautiful voice. He lay in wait for the children from the local national school to learn their latest songs, and it was extraordinary to hear that remarkable old man, whose sense of music and language were impeccable, imitating the metronomic beat and the synthetic accent that the school children had picked up – a horrifying example of what we do to ancient cultures when we try to revive them.

However, he did sing the song, and I got it down as well as I could, while he interrupted me to point out some verbal felicity. The first verse begins 'One lovely evening at the yellowing of the

sun', and he stopped and cried, 'There's a beautiful phrase for you
– "the yellowing of the sun". There's a cartload of meaning in
that – *Tá lán trucaill de bhrí annsan.*'

I had brought whiskey and the Tailor provided beer, and as we
left Batty Kit threw his arms round my neck and sobbed, 'Thanks
be to God, Frinshias, we had one grand dirty night.' Then, as we
went up the mountain road in the moonlight, Traynor stopped
and looked back.

'Now they're beginning to talk about us,' he said darkly.

'Let them,' I said, but I knew that he was haunted by the
thought that whenever he was not there Life in some unimagin-
ably interesting way was going on.

Then came a tragedy that none of us had expected. A young
chemist from London who was camping in Gougane Barra
became friendly with the Tailor and made an enchanting record
of his conversation and stories to which I wrote an introduction.
Mr Edward de Valera's government immediately banned it as
being 'in its general tendency indecent and obscene'. It was a
staggering blow for that kind old couple, who had no notion of
how their simple country jokes and pieties would be regarded by
illiterate city upstarts. The scores of students who had accepted
their hospitality affected never to have heard of them. Their
neighbours boycotted them; all but the sergeant of the local police
who cycled out regularly to see that they were not interfered with.
Three louts of priests called and forced the old man to go on his
knees before his own hearth and burn his copy of the book.

The tailor found one defender in a Protestant landlord, Sir
John Keane, who spoke of him in the Senate. But the government
henchmen would have none of it, and Mr de Valera's friend
Senator Bill Magennis made a speech in which he referred to
Ansty as 'a moron'.

It was almost as hard on Traynor as it was on the old couple, for
his position as a priest made it impossible for him to speak out. He
and I visited them together. Nobody from the neighbourhood
called, but the Tailor made light of it all. In fact I rarely heard him
talk so well. When we rose to go, we found that some local

hooligans had rammed the branch of a tree between the latch and the wall so that we were imprisoned until someone got through the little cottage window and released us. Ansty, dreading that the hooligans intended to burn them alive in their home, began to sob, and the Tailor patted her gently and said, 'There, there, girl! At our age there is little more the world can do to us.'

Years later, the Irish government appointed an Appeal Board, which instantly discovered that *The Tailor and Ansty* was neither indecent nor obscene, but by that time the book was out of print and the Tailor and Ansty were dead, so it was all quite proper and perfectly safe.

Traynor died while I was in America, and somehow or other his priest friends managed to bury him where he had always wished to be buried, in Gougane Barra: how, I don't know for, being Traynor, he died penniless and intestate; the rules dictated that he should be buried in the town, and the island cemetery he wished to be buried in had been closed by order of the bishop.

But even in death he was a romantic, bending circumstances to his will, and his old friends brought him there on Little Christmas Night, when the snow was on the mountains, and the country people came across the dangerous rocks and streams with their lanterns, and an array of cars turned their headlights on the causeway to the island church where he was to spend his last night above ground.

At the other side of the causeway lies the Tailor, under the noble headstone carved for him by his friend Seamus Murphy, with the epitaph I chose for him – 'A star danced and under it I was born'. I was glad that Traynor permitted that, though he refused to allow Murphy to do what he wanted and replace the cross with an open shears. He himself has no gravestone, but the country people have not forgotten him and on his grave his initials are picked out in little coloured stones. Even in death the things that Traynor would have most liked to know have been hidden from him.

16

IN 1937, two years after Russell's death, I had a dress rehearsal of the death that had haunted me from the time I was a child. For years Father had been nagging at me in his own quiet way to get hold of Mother's birth certificate. At last, he wrote me a peremptory letter, and off I went, half angry, half amused, to the Custom House and wasted time searching for the entry of her birth where I felt it ought to be until I found it more or less where Father said it should be – seventy years back, all but a month or so. I was slightly shocked and very sad, because I had never thought her old at all, but she didn't seem to take it personally. 'Your poor Dad will be so pleased,' she said thoughtfully, evoking a very clear picture of Father's boyish pride and the excitement with which he would report it to the family and friends.

She was staying with me at the time, and for the first birthday party she would remember I brought home a bottle of champagne. I should have had sense enough to realize the effect that even a glass of sherry could have on her. After supper I went for my usual walk. When I came home she was in the kitchen and she rushed out to greet me. Between the hall door and the kitchen there were seven or eight steps and before my eyes she tripped and tumbled down into the hallway at my feet. When I tried to lift her she moaned, and I realized that she was badly injured. The McGarrys, who owned the house I lived in, carried her to bed and telephoned for Hayes. I was no help to them because I was hysterical. It seemed to me unbelievable coincidence that she should die after her first birthday party, and I blamed myself and my damned champagne.

Hayes arrived soon after and spent nearly half an hour in her room. I waited in the hall, and when he came out I saw from his look that he had no hope. He put his arm about me and drew me into the front room, shutting the door behind him. 'It's easier for you to hear this from me than from someone else,' he said gently. 'I'm afraid she isn't going to live. Her shoulder and pelvis are broken, and I've never known an elderly person who survived it. Even if she did, she'd never walk again. All the same, she is a remarkable woman, and I'd be happier if we could get a specialist to see her. It's late, but if I can get Charlie Macauley on the phone he may come. Charlie was very attached to his own mother.'

Macauley was at home and came out immediately. While we waited for him, Hayes said: 'It's extraordinary. Do you realize that that woman has had chronic appendicitis since she was a girl, and never even told a doctor about it.' Macauley confirmed Hayes' opinion and advised me not to expect the impossible. He insisted on getting her into a nursing home immediately, and about midnight the ambulance took her to one in Eccles Street. I walked home through the dark streets, knowing I should not sleep. I had to break the news to Father yet, and I knew he would blame me, as I blamed myself. And what made it hardest was to think of the stoicism with which she had all her life borne the pain of chronic appendicitis, knowing she could not afford to go to a doctor or take the time to enter a hospital.

When I saw her next day Mother was still resigned to death, but she had got some very interesting stories from the nurses. On the following day she complained that she looked a sight and that the nurses could not do her hair, so I combed and brushed it for her. 'A private room in a nursing home,' she said, closing her eyes, 'sure it must be costing a fortune', and anyhow, even from bed, she could look after me better than I could do for myself. I met Macauley outside her room and told him. 'The funny thing is, she probably will go home,' he said. 'At this very moment I'm looking after a girl patient who did exactly the same thing to herself on the hunting field, and she'll never walk again.' It was ten days before Mother did come home, and then the McGarrys gave up their beautiful drawing-room on the ground floor to her. But she was very embarrassed at having to wear a dressing-gown when she went to and from the bathroom. 'My goodness,' she said, 'you could meet anybody in that hall.' After that, the dressing-gown was put away, and I had to dress and undress her as well as brush and put up her hair.

Meanwhile I had arranged to take my holiday in Switzerland, to see a specialist on my own account – a famous doctor who had been a friend of Thomas Mann at Davos – but Minnie Connolly's letters from Cork were alarming. Father, well-informed by me about the gravity of the situation, had chosen it as an excuse for an uproarious drunk. I knew what life with him would be like while Mother couldn't even climb a stair, much less go out to the pub to 'get it' for him. Instead, I took her with me to Switzerland. The journey, of course, was an intolerable chore. Mother was much too modest to look for the 'Ladies' herself; I had to find it and lead her to it. And, like all chores for her, it turned into joy. Mother made an intimate friend of the chambermaid in the London hotel, and got her life story from a nice girl she had chummed up with in Trafalgar Square. She disliked Paris, because no one could tell her any interesting life stories. Besides, she hated French coffee and broke into tears on me when I took her up to the Basilica in Montmartre and bought her some. However, Switzerland made up for it, and she liked to sit on the terrace of the hotel and listen to the crowds yodelling on the little pleasure boats passing up and down from Geneva and to go on the funicular to some little mountain chapel where she could say her prayers and listen to the cow-bells tinkling in the evening. She also made friends with a Swiss lady who spoke excellent English and was good enough to tell her the story of her life. It was all much more like home.

She cramped my style, for I had intended when I was finished with the doctor to tramp over one of the passes into Italy as Irish pilgrims had done in the seventh and eighth centuries, but still I felt a sort of enchantment in the holiday. It was like the fulfilment of a prophecy, the accidental keeping of promises made to her as a small boy, when she came in exhausted by a hard day's work and I airily described to her – all out of a guide-book and a couple of phrase-books – the wonderful journeys we should make when I was older and had come into my own. And the enchantment was only sharpened by the feeling of guilt we both had when we worried about my foolish father staggering home to Harrington's Square when the public-houses shut.

Father survived Mother's absence, but on her return he made it clear that he thought I had had more than my share of her. Life in Harrington Square was restored to its rigid pattern more firmly than ever, despite Mother's wistful reminiscences of the continent. It was some years before the occasion Father had been looking forward to for so long occurred, and I found myself responsible for a woman and her son, waiting for the end of ecclesiastical and divorce court proceedings so that I could marry. Of course, I had been asking for that. You can't live on two levels – the level of the imagination in what concerns yourself and the level of reason in what concerns others – for sooner or later the two will change places; and no consideration of expediency had ever really deterred me from getting into situations which my experience did not qualify me to deal with. Every humiliation that can be inflicted on a man who tries to live by his imagination and doesn't know the rules of the group to which he aspires I had gone through, and this was merely the greatest of them.

Mother came to stay and was reassured, as I knew she would be, for she could deal with any situation, no matter how preposterous from her point of view, so long as she could size it up for herself. After she went back, it was Father's turn, because somehow or other my life would not have been complete unless he had seen me in my new part as a father myself. I think now that perhaps I built too much on that; perhaps I always built too much on his visits, hoping each time that at last things between us would be as they should have been from the start and that I could confide in him things I could not have confided even in Mother. When I rushed to open the carriage door for him, he staggered out, very drunk. He must have been all right before he left home or Mother would have kept him there, but he had had a long wait at Waterford for a connection, and boredom or nervousness had proved too much for him.

I got him home and put him to bed, but not before the child had seen him. I knew the boy's look because it had been my own at his age, and faced with this disaster I wasn't a day older than he. I knew I couldn't control Father; nobody could control him when he was like that, and I lay awake, shivering as if in a fever and going through the whole nightmare of my childhood again. I must have fallen asleep, for in the early hours of the morning I found he had got out, and knew what had happened. He was rambling mad through the countryside, looking for a public-house and hammering at the door for drink. Later I went to search for him and when I found him said, 'This can't go on. I have trouble enough in this place already.' 'I know, I know,' he muttered stupidly. 'I shouldn't have come. I'll go back by the next train. I'll be better at home.' 'I'm afraid you will,' I said, and later that day saw him off from the little station. My heart was torn with pity and remorse because I knew that was no way to behave to a dog, let alone to someone you loved, and yet I could not control the childish terror and hatred that he had instilled into me so long ago when he threw us out in our night clothes on the street, or attacked Mother with an open razor.

I never saw him again. A few weeks later war broke out and communications collapsed. What was worse for people of Father's generation, tea was rationed to a fraction of what people in Britain were allowed, and when he wasn't on the booze he had nothing else to drink. It was part of the poverty of our class that we grew up literally on bread and tea and never felt really hungry if we had enough of both. Mother and Father did what the rest of their generation did and left the tea-leaves in the pot to be watered again and again till the last colouring had gone from them. When I worried about it, it wasn't of Mother but of him I was thinking, for apart from liquor he had no other resource.

He died as he had lived, blundering drunk about Cork in the last stages of pneumonia, sustained by nothing but his giant physique (my cousin Christy, who looked after him, told me at the funeral about the big black stain that appeared about his heart when he died). Mother refused to tell me anything until he was dead. This was something I found hard to forgive, because though with half her mind she felt she was saving me anxiety, deep down there was something else, not far removed from resentment – the feeling that I wouldn't understand and that I never had understood. She was like a loving woman who, when her husband has been unfaithful to her, blames not the husband, but the other woman. 'That damned drink!' she would cry bitterly, always implying that it was the drink that followed Father, not Father the drink, and in this she was probably wiser than I. But she felt that only she could have the patience to deal with him when he was dying and to realize that he must be allowed to die in his own way, not mine, as in later years she followed him with Masses and prayers, knowing as no one else could know, how lost and embarrassed that shy, home-keeping man would be with no Minnie O'Connor to come home to, no home, no Cork, no pension, astray in the infinite wastes of eternity.

PART THREE

THE ABBEY THEATRE

17

LENNOX Robinson, who at Corkery's request had given me my first job, had been a director of the Abbey Theatre since Lady Gregory's day. It was against Robinson that F. R. Higgins intrigued so passionately, although Robinson was a much better intriguer than Higgins himself, and, in the beginning at least, much closer to Yeats. When I knew Yeats first and would visit him at his home, Robinson frequently strolled in towards the end of an evening to report on how the play at the Abbey was doing and how much had been taken at the box office. Usually the children refused to go to sleep until Robinson had come to say good-night to them, and children do not feel like that towards a man unless he is a good one.

Robinson was very good to me. Although he had been tight about my wages when he took me on as an assistant librarian, he made up for it when I came to Dublin almost as a stranger. He took me to the Abbey with him, let me sit in on rehearsals and introduced me to the players. Occasionally he invited me to spend the night with him. He lived in a small house on the shore of Dublin Bay with his mother, a sweet old lady from County Cork, who was glad to talk, even to a papist, about places and people she knew there. She called Robinson 'Stuart' (his real name was Esmé Stuart Lennox, in memory of some remote Scottish ancestor), and it was clear that Stuart to her was an entirely different person from this lanky, remote, melancholy man who kissed her good-night at ten o'clock and then brought out the whiskey decanter and drank himself stupid before morning.

He had been something of a musician, and when the whiskey was lowered and the French window open on the rocks over the strand, he would play his gramophone. He mocked me in his brilliant, bitter way, because I was uneducated and did not really admire any music but that of the three or four composers I knew well. He would deliberately play music he knew I would not like, but sometimes we came to an understanding over *Der Rosenkavalier* or American folk songs, to both of which he introduced me. I was unaccustomed to alcohol and completely unaccustomed to late hours, and often the dawn was breaking over Dublin Bay when the pair of us staggered up to bed.

I admired him enormously, but never became fond of him. I could not understand the sudden, extraordinary changes of mood, when the kind adviser turned into a mean, sardonic enemy, determined on making every word rankle. With Phibbs I could answer back, and our quarrels only resulted in a deeper friendship, but I stood too much in awe of Robinson to answer him back.

I had admired his later work and produced it in Cork without realizing that a footnote like 'If this play is produced in England, read Birmingham instead of Cork' was not really a Kafkaian generalization of the theme, but a desperate appeal for a London production. I had not learned then that in literature X never marks the spot.

When I knew him first, Yeats had what I can only call a 'crush' on Lennox Robinson, whom he insisted on calling 'Lennix'. One of Robinson's 'functional' plays – 'a table, two chairs and a passion' as the author described it – had been slighted in England, and Yeats insisted on reviving it in Dublin, with a programme note by himself, trouncing the English critics. 'Within five years Lennix will be a European figure,' Yeats assured me with a wave of his hand, and I was glad to report the confidence to Robinson. I had not counted on the depth of despondency in him, because he merely looked away and said drearily, 'He might as well have said five hundred.' One morning, before we went to bed, we strolled down the garden to look at the first streaks of dawn on Dublin Bay, and Robinson said with his usual Regency emphasis: 'One *night* I shall swim out into *that*, and swim and *swim* until I give up.' It sounded to me like the whiskey, and unfortunately for himself it was the whiskey.

My memory seems to have made a blank of all that conversation of his, sometimes silly, but often delightful. Even free whiskey doesn't make bores tolerable, and Robinson had his own profundities. Once, when we had the usual argument about the early and late O'Casey, in which I must have been at fault, he suddenly burst out, 'I don't *mind* how many bad plays Sean writes for the rest of his life. What*ever* they may be like, they will be the plays of a happy man.' That stuck in my memory, not only because of its relevance to O'Casey – and it is very relevant to O'Casey – but because of its relevance to himself. It is the remark of a man who will never be happy again.

Yeats was for ever probing me about him. He knew that I admired Robinson as he did, and felt that I was keeping from him things he should know. There was that dedication of a book to Iseult Gonne, which suggested an unhappy love affair, but by this time we both felt that Robinson was only pretending to be in love with Iseult because Yeats had been in love with her. 'What *is* wrong with Lennix,' he asked me point-blank one night, and, remembering the conversation overlooking Dublin Bay in the dawn, I said, 'Dissatisfaction with his work.' Yeats looked at me shrewdly over his glasses and said, 'I was afraid you were going to say dissatisfaction with something else.' I think he knew what the something else was, and, while resenting my refusal to confide in him, liked me just a little bit better for it. I felt that he thought for the most part that Catholics were not to be trusted, but on the odd occasions when we hit it off he began to develop a theory that I was really the illegitimate son of some Protestant big house.

Meanwhile, the Abbey Theatre was going rapidly to the dogs. After the death of Lady Gregory, Yeats had allowed it to pass entirely into the control of Robinson. After her first experience of him as a young man Lady Gregory allowed him no control whatever, because she thought him irresponsible about money and morbid in his attitude to life. She made no bones about her dislike for him, and he would hardly have remained on as a director of the theatre if it had not been for Yeats. He took his revenge by editing her journals and choosing all the biting things she said of him for quotation to his friends. But that brilliant, moody, despondent man was a dead weight on the theatre. It wasn't only that he drank himself, he encouraged the younger actors to drink with him. He not only approved of dreary farces, but when a fine play came in he would fasten on some fault and try to have the play rejected. As his own circumstances grew worse, he grew more and more obstructive.

The theatre was heavily in debt. It was keeping open only on the strength of a group of favourite knockabout comedies by Robinson himself, Brinsley MacNamara and George Shiels, excellent comedies, some of them, but all produced in the same slapdash hearty manner as though they were all written by the same author. If it had not been for the players – and there was hardly a weak actor in the group – the Abbey might not have survived. In Barry Fitzgerald (William Shields) it had a great comedian, in Maureen Delaney a great comedienne; F. J. McCormick and Eileen Crowe were two of the best actors I have ever seen. Any play that suited their genius did not even have to be completely written. They could do almost anything they pleased with a part. I once saw Fitzgerald set a scene of astounding bitterness in a comedy of Shiels and turn it into an uproarious farce. Usually the players directed themselves – sometimes they even selected the plays that were to be performed – and one got the impression of a garden gone wild, of every player grown so tall that it was all but impossible to tell what a play was really like. It was not the players' fault. I have never forgotten one performance of Synge's *Playboy of the Western World* in which all the wild Connemara girls appeared in permanent waves.

According to Robinson, the old plays had to be put on all the time because there were no new ones. I didn't believe him, because in a theatre, as in a magazine, you get exactly what you look for. Theatre directors, like editors, must go out and find their writers, and W. B. Yeats was too old now to forage on his own. Yet, although he didn't want to let Robinson down, Yeats was not happy with Robinson's excuses. Once, when I was talking with Yeats about *The Saint and Mary Kate*, which I was writing at the time, he said wistfully, 'I wish you would write that as a play for me.' Had he been George Russell I probably would have tried to, for I realized a great Editor like Russell would have handled the situation so differently. 'My dear boy, that is a play, not a novel. Now the first date available is November 10th, which means that we have to start rehearsals not later than October 15th, so if you can let me have a script within the next month I can guarantee you a production.'

And yet I am sure that Robinson was quite sincere. Though his inertia and indifference meant that his own harmless plays were kept permanently in the repertory, and though later I saw him try to ditch the work of better writers, either by faint praise or by criticism that smacked of dishonesty, I think his real weakness as a director was that he was himself in a state of despondency, and no despondent man can do work that requires endless improvisation. That was the 'morbid' streak in him of which Lady Gregory had been afraid. When Fred Higgins took his place as Yeats' best friend, Robinson's position became pitiable, and by 1935 Higgins had already achieved the first stage in his attempt to dislodge him.

Meanwhile, across the street from the Abbey two enthusiastic penniless young actors from London, Mícheál MacLiammóir and Hilton Edwards, were filling their little theatre, the Gate, with productions of European classics like Brand, Peer Gynt and Anna Christie. When anyone mentioned their success, Yeats was furious. 'Anything Edwards and MacLiammóir can do, Lennix and Dolly' (later Mrs Robinson) 'can do better,' he told me, but he didn't really believe it. He reconstituted the Board of Directors of the Abbey and brought on Higgins, Brinsley MacNamara and Ernest Blythe, the ex-Minister for Finance to whom the theatre owed its little subsidy of eight hundred pounds. The last appointment was typical of Yeats, who never forgot a rebuke or an obligation.

But the eight hundred pounds a year gave the Irish government the right to appoint its own representative on the Board. The Cosgrave governments had exercised this right discreetly by appointing people like George O'Brien and Walter Starkie, of whom Yeats approved; but de Valera's government refused to reappoint Starkie and appointed instead a notorious and unscrupulous politician named Magennis. Yeats, who knew the man of old (everyone in Dublin seemed to know Magennis of old), reappointed Starkie as an ordinary member of the Board, refused to sanction the government nominee and threatened to close the theatre instead. He then learned that before being offered to Magennis the seat had been offered to and refused by Hayes in his usual petulant way. Yeats rushed round to my flat to ask me to intercede with Hayes to withdraw his refusal. By this time I knew enough about Hayes' vanity to realize that the appeal would be much more effective if Yeats himself made it, and we took a taxi to Hayes' house in Sandymount.

Hayes' manners were even more formal than Yeats', and when I introduced them there was a pretty competition in elegance, which I enjoyed. Yeats made a brief, passionate speech, appealing to Hayes on behalf of his theatre. It was only one of the many I heard him make, yet it was only when he was dead that I realized how urgent they all were. He was appealing for something that to him was perhaps the most important part of his life's work, something that must be passed on to future generations as he, Synge and Lady Gregory had fashioned it.

Hayes rose and stood before the fire with his hands behind his back.

'Mr Yeats,' he said loftily, 'I have no interest in the theatre. I have no knowledge of the theatre. I can be of no help to you there, but if I can be of any assistance to you in keeping that ruffian out, I shall be glad to accept.'

So 'that ruffian' was bought off with a seat in the Senate, which carried a salary, where later he was de Valera's principal spokesman in the attack on the old Tailor of Gougane Barra and his wife. Through my friendship with Hayes I became an intimate observer of the workings of a theatre which I had attacked again and again and whose policy I disapproved of.

I had also, without realizing it, put a large nail in the coffin of Yeats' life work.

The new Board, to show how up-to-date it was, decided to compete with Edwards and MacLiammóir by producing European classics also. I doubt if it ever crossed their minds that what attracted younger people like myself to that pair of rascals was not that they had discovered the key to wealth, but that they were nearly as crazy as Yeats himself had been in his youth and produced what they wanted to produce regardless of anyone's opinion.

So the first thing the new Board did, just as Hayes joined it, was to import a young English director named Hugh Hunt and a young English stage designer called Tanya Moiseiwitsch, to balance Edwards and MacLiammóir, and set them to producing a rigmarole of 'European' plays like *Noah*, *Coriolanus* and *Dr Faustus*. Meanwhile, Robinson went on with his productions of Irish plays, though he did take over from Hunt a scurvy piece of French religiosity about St Ignatius Loyola. The division shows a split personality on the Board, though I suspect that the split was in Yeats rather than in the Board, which did not seem to have any particular personality to split. Yeats prided himself on his sublety, though as theatre manager he was very unhappy. If the current of opinion was in favour of European masterpieces – which bored him – he would have European masterpieces, but he would not have any damn English director tinkering with the sort of plays that had been written by himself, Synge and Lady Gregory, and producing them in a theatrical idiom he did not like. Though he was responsible for Mrs Pat Campbell, his whole attitude to English directors and players could be summed up in Synge's comment on Mrs Pat as Deirdre of the Sorrows: 'She'll turn it into The Second Mrs Conchobhar.' The theatre now had two producers, though it could not afford to pay the salary of one.

However, the new policy had scarcely been announced than Brinsley MacNamara, in a fit of pique, issued a personal pronunciamento against O'Casey, the greatest of contemporary Irish dramatists, and the other members of the Board in another fit of pique demanded his resignation. They invited me to take his place, and though I admired MacNamara as the ablest of the directors, after Yeats, and thought the Board's attitude to him absurd, I agreed. I entered the Boardroom for the first time, seeing nothing but the figures of John Synge and Augusta Gregory, and trusting they would inspire me, but their inspiration was similar to that of the Sacred Heart and the Blessed Virgin in earlier days when I couldn't do my lessons or my work.

I knew nothing about the theatre, and so asked the advice of my best friend among the players, Arthur Shields, as to what I should do, and his advice was so extraordinary that I took it as a good joke until I noticed that I was creating chaos in the theatre. 'Treat us as though we were children,' he said shortly. 'Nice children, of course; children that you're fond of, but not as grown-ups. And for God's sake, whatever you do, don't praise us. That drives us mad.' It is the best advice that was ever given to a man of the theatre, if only he could be intelligent enough to appreciate it. I wasn't; not for a long time. Arthur never made a great reputation as an actor; he was far too discerning for that; and it was only when I had almost wrecked the company that I realized how discerning he was.

18

FOR much of the time during his last years Yeats did not attend meetings of the Abbey Board at all. Either he was abroad or he was at home and didn't feel strong enough to face the trip into town. Initially, not being observant, I got the impression that he was only vaguely interested. I should have remembered the evenings at his home when Robinson dropped in late to report on the takings and the other evening when Higgins had telephoned him after the meeting of the Academy of Letters to report on what O'Faolain and I had said. The old watchdog never relaxed his vigilance, and after every Board meeting Higgins called, telephoned or wrote to recount every word that had been said – rarely in a favourable way, if I knew Higgins.

Yeats was one of the most devious men I have ever known, and I deliberately mocked at his deviousness as he mocked at my simple-mindedness, probably with equal justification. He was taken aback at the trustfulness I showed towards my fellow-directors, and he once hinted as much to me. 'Well, I can't treat them as if they were a gang of masked conspirators,' I said irritably, and he replied with great unction, 'No, you remind me of a character in a Victorian novel by a lady that I once read – someone who believes that for most of the time the vast majority of people do not intend much harm to the others.' That description of my own character delighted me so much that I didn't even notice the pinch till I got home. In the light of later events he was putting it mildly.

The best example of his deviousness I remember was in the last year of his life, at a time when I felt that at last he and I were on the point of an understanding. By this time, like the two kings in *The*

Herne's Egg, we had fought so long and so hard that there didn't seem to be much left to us except to become close friends. Paul Vincent Carroll had written a play which offended some members of the Board, and, instead of sending it along to Yeats and me in the ordinary way, they had returned the play to the author with an exceedingly insulting letter. When the Secretary showed me the letter I grew furiously angry. Quite apart from the fact that Carroll was a distinguished playwright who had earned a good deal of money for the theatre, I felt that no writer should be treated with such discourtesy, so I wrote to Carroll, asking him to submit the play again to Yeats and myself. He did so, and Yeats and I did not meet again until the Board meeting at which our two reports were read out. Yeats said, 'All the characters in this play are corrugated iron', but he went on in his noble way to praise Carroll's work and volunteered to contribute fifty pounds from his own pocket (a lot of money for an old man who made manuscript copies of *Innisfree* for American booksellers at five pounds a time) towards its production by Edwards and MacLiammóir at the Gate or any other theatre that wanted to produce it. My report read, 'All the characters in this play are cardboard', and Yeats started and stared incredulously at me. Then, as my negative report went on, he began to chuckle grimly, and when it concluded he said, 'O'Connor, I owe you an apology. I thought you'd asked the play back because Carroll was a friend of yours. It had not occurred to me that you had asked it back because you thought he had been unfairly treated. It serves me right! I've lost my fifty pounds.' How could anyone not love the sort of man who said a thing like that?

Still, in the matter of deviousness, he was a child compared with Higgins. Even as I wrote down this fairly straightforward story I found myself wondering, 'Who or what gave Yeats the notion that I was a friend of Carroll's; above all, a friend who, right or wrong, would insist on the production of his play?' Twenty times at least I had evidence that Higgins told Yeats things that simply weren't true. Why had it not occurred to me that this might be another of them? The truth is that Higgins created such a miasma of intrigue about him that I look back on it as I used to look at Abbey plays of the period, wondering what exactly was going on behind it all.

Most of the time Hayes made an admirable director, warm-hearted, appreciative and intelligent. I paid no attention to the old-maidish tizzies into which he worked himself occasionally about a scene or a word – generally concerning politics or religion. Usually he could be kidded out of them. Walter Starkie, the ex-government representative whom Yeats had brought on under his own steam, was a fat amiable man, as amiable as Higgins, but with none of Higgins' intolerable treachery. Starkie took little part in meetings or discussion, although once – it was the time of the Civil War in Spain – when I came into the Boardroom late with an evening paper and said, 'Well, boys, we've got the Alcazar', he became very voluble. 'Really,' he said, 'I cannot understand how people who know nothing of Spain can speak like that of this terrible Civil War.' (He later became the British Council representative to Madrid.) Robinson had what no other Board member had, an immense capacity for silent, despondent resistance. He merely sat back in his chair, sucked his pipe and replied in monosyllables. If I had known that Ernest Blythe was the man who would outlast us all I should have paid more attention to him than I did. He looked like a Buddha in grey plaster, and spent most of his time doodling on his pad. Then someone would use a specialized polysyllabic word and im-mediately a great change came over Blythe. Pencil poised on paper, he waited for inspiration, and then would write down a Gaelic equivalent. Then there was a further pause and he wrote down an alternative. He was genuinely attached to the Irish language and anxious to revive it, but in his wise way he realized that it was lacking in polysyllabic words. He believed that the language could be revived if only people could be induced to sing popular songs in it. His collected poems contain his translation of 'The Beautiful Isle of Capri' and American songs like 'I Got a Gal in Kalamazoo' in his peculiar version of the Irish language. One might call Blythe a single-minded man if the adjective did not raise the question of whether or not it was a contradiction in terms.

Hugh Hunt got off on the wrong foot by wearing a red, white and blue rosette in the theatre on some English state occasion (King George V's jubilee I imagine), which infuriated Higgins. Higgins' dislike of Hunt had turned to a persecution mania when Hunt gave an interview to some English weekly paper in which he spoke of his difficulties and described Higgins and myself as red revolutionaries, determined on turning the theatre towards our own political aims. Higgins, having at last unmasked a genuine plot, demanded his immediate dismissal; Hayes was fearfully upset because he didn't want 'that charming boy' dismissed over an indiscretion. I had conceived an admiration for Hunt that has outlasted our theatrical relationship, and was delighted at Hunt's display of independence. When he came before the Board to explain that he had never said those dreadful things – and I'm sure they were exaggerated in the news report – I interrupted to say that of course he had, but in future would he mind not saying them before newspapermen.

At the same time I found myself engaged in a long battle with Robinson which was to go on until I resigned. I had come on the Board as his friend, but it didn't take long to realize that the theatre had been mismanaged for years and that most of the mismanagement could be traced to him. When the bank threatened to close down the theatre, he merely shrugged and said, 'Every theatre in the world carries an overdraft.' We had two producers, Robinson for Irish plays and Hunt for European ones, and two secretaries, Eric Gorman for correspondence and Robinson's brother, Tom, for accounts. The presence of Robinson's brother at Board meetings made another difficulty, for it meant that even when Robinson was absent there could be no confidential criticism of his work. The directors groused among themselves, but nothing was ever said at meetings. I asked for the exclusion of Robinson's brother from Board meetings. Soon afterwards his appointment was terminated. I regretted it, but it was difficult to see how else we were to save the Abbey. Then the company shares were redistributed to deprive Robinson of the controlling interest he would have when Yeats died.

Higgins, of course, was the most pugnacious member of our Board and criticized me to Yeats and Yeats to me and Robinson and Hunt to anyone who would listen; but he could not fight. He saw secret agents everywhere, but the vivid imagination that had created them collapsed the moment they presented themselves before him in ordinary human shapes, and at the least sign of opposition his astute criticisms turned into jokes. His very amiability prevented his fighting. I had no ability as an intriguer and could be fooled by appearances most of the time, so I had no shyness about fighting for any reasonable cause. Higgins made no secret of the fact that he used me as his muscle man – just as the Board used me in that capacity to have the shares redistributed and have Robinson's brother removed from the room during meetings. Once, reporting in shouts of laughter to the Board how he got rid of some importunate playwright, he said, 'I use O'Connor all the time as an excuse. You have no idea of the character that man has in Dublin! Murphy showed me his play and I couldn't read it, so I told him it was a masterpiece, and then, when he kept persecuting me, I said O'Connor had turned it down. They'll believe anything of him.' He enacted these scenes with such laughter and devilment that only an out-and-out egotist could have complained, but now I wonder whether the joke was not on me and Yeats.

The New Abbey Policy of competing with Edwards and MacLiammóir I disagreed with on two grounds. One was that it seemed to require two producers when we couldn't afford one. The other and more important reason was that, in my view, it was wrong. For years the directors had been unable to find new Irish plays, or so they said, or so Robinson had persuaded them, and later, when really interesting new plays were submitted, the Board had practically decided beforehand that the plays could be no good. Even when it was working at full capacity the theatre never managed to produce more than a half-dozen new plays a year. I felt that this could be increased to nine or ten, but, allowing for the fact that some of them would have to be popular plays by established playwrights like Robinson himself, Shields and MacNamara, the production of four or five European classics like *Coriolanus* and *Dr Faustus* would mean that there would be no opportunity for young serious dramatists. This would mean the end of the literary movement, for magazine and book publishers we had none.

As for the European classics, I had seen them performed as well as I was ever to do and had decided that they might not be as classical as they were generally supposed to be. Shakespeare could be boring, so could Sheridan; one could even get too much of Ibsen and Chekhov. I had not yet classified them as 'Museum Theatre', and in those days would probably have disputed the theory. The theory I later evolved to explain my own disillusionment I have expounded so often that I have almost ceased to believe in it myself. It seemed to me that the theatre is by its nature a contemporary art, a collaboration between author, players and audience, and once the collaboration is broken down by time it cannot be repeated.

There are exceptions, of course, particularly when an old text is rehandled by a modern writer and the staging re-created in terms of a contemporary society. Even with *Hamlet* one can still enable the audience to walk on the razor's edge of real drama, but in my experience it was much easier to make them walk it with some little play by a contemporary author in a local setting. The lightest of Robinson's own comedies had an immediacy of effect that Goethe's *Faust* or Ibsen's *Peer Gynt* at the rival theatre did not have. If I was to work for it, the Abbey had to be an all-Irish theatre.

Yeats, too, of course, wanted a living theatre. If he had been younger and in better health he would have come to the theatre himself and insisted on it. It was he who in the middle of the New Abbey Policy was desperately holding on to Lennox Robinson and a few rough and ready comedies, so that when he died he might transmit some part of what he and his friends had achieved in the creation of an original repertory and an original style of acting. Nowadays when I think of what the situation really was, it is not of my work and feelings that I think, but of his. Like many a lesser man who has created some unique institution, he wanted to guarantee its continuance when he himself was dead, and did not realize that what he wanted was a miracle. His sense of urgency is evident in the dispute over the production of *Coriolanus*. It had just been produced in Paris in coloured shirts and caused a riot. Yeats demanded that we produce it in coloured shirts among our European classics, in the hope that, as in France, a Dublin audience might riot and he could defend the message of the play as he had defended the message of *The Playboy of the Western World* and *The Plough and the Stars*.

I don't think he understood that I admired the tradition as much as he did, but in the circumstances of the theatre I thought he was going the wrong way about saving it. *Coriolanus* might be a dramatic gesture, but there is a difference between that and drama. Besides, with Spain bleeding to death, my judgment as a theatre man was influenced by not wanting to have any part in Fascist propaganda. I refused to agree to its being produced in coloured shirts, so Hunt finally produced the play in Renaissance costume. This saved a riot maybe, but it lost the theatre a lot of money, and I practically finished the job of bankrupting it.

After that, the New Abbey Policy was not heard of again till I went to the first performance of a nice little play about the poet James Clarence Mangan, and saw a Masque of the Seven Deadly Sins, which had not been in the original manuscript. I realized that Hunt simply could not stand those beautiful and expensive masks that had been made for *Dr Faustus* lying around unused, and had induced the author to write a scene about them. Poor Mangan! Later, when I came to write a study of *Macbeth*, this enabled me to understand why Macbeth's death scene had been omitted and his head brought in on a pole instead. The stage director of Shakespeare's company had a head available, as we had masks for the Seven Deadly Sins. Theatre people are like that – even Hunt. Not economical – definitely not economical – but very conscious that use can be made of the stuff that is lying about the theatre.

Meanwhile, though Robinson had blown cold on our two best plays – Carroll's *Shadow and Substance* and Teresa Deevy's *Katie Roche* – we produced new plays and recovered lost ground. I had gone the rounds begging for plays and had a few promises, one from Sean O'Faolain and another from Brinsley MacNamara. Then Hunt had the idea of dramatizing a story of mine called 'In the Train', and, with the threat of *Dr Faustus* hanging over me I jumped at the chance. I disliked Hunt's method of dramatization, which had choruses in the manner of a German impressionist play, with invisible groups chanting in the rhythm of the train, 'To Stop the Train Pull Down the Chain – PULL – DOWN – THE – CHAIN – *Pull Down the Chain*.' But the performance proved that Hunt was the very man we needed to put new life into the tradition. The curtain went up and there was an Irish railway carriage, lovingly re-created in every particular, and a group of Irish villagers – not Abbey comics – who were involved in a murder trial the significance of which they could not apprehend. The whole performance was drawn to a fourth of the scale usual in Abbey productions, but every detail was in focus and exquisitely rendered, and one could hear from the audience little chuckles of delighted recognition, as when one of the policemen pulled down his great-coat to use as a card table. The most beautiful performance was that by Denis O'Dea, whose voice and build have kept him cast as the stage Irish policeman, and who there, for a few minutes, created a gentle timid country boy in uniform that I have never been able to forget. I knew that night that Hunt could give us the thing I had dreamed of for years, a theatre that could express the poetic realism that I admired in Liam O'Flaherty, Sean O'Faolain and Peadar O'Donnell.

As I rushed round to the green-room to congratulate the players I bumped into Yeats, who was equally excited, but for a different reason. 'O'Connor, you have made a *terrible* mistake. You should have explained in the first scene that the woman was the murderess. You must never, NEVER, keep a secret from your audience.' He said it in the tone of an American television announcer telling you you may never drive a car without consulting your local agent, but though I fancy I swore under my breath, I knew he was right again. Fictional irony and dramatic irony have nothing in common. It was one of the occasions when I got a hint of what a really great man of the theatre Yeats was, far greater than Robinson, who had the reputation.

Yeats had a fixation on the well-made play, and the functional type of production which he passed on to Robinson. 'A play is two chairs and a passion,' Robinson would quote, and Yeats went one better by quoting enthusiastically a story of Salvini. Salvini was rehearsing on a stage that was empty but for one chair, and finally he could stand it no longer and asked, 'When do I break the chair?' I saw Yeats' original production of his own translation of *Oedipus Rex*, in which Oedipus hardly changed his position from beginning to end of the play, and for once I wanted to scream. Years later I saw Laurence Olivier's production of the same version, and Laurence, remembering that 'Oedipus' means 'clubfoot', demonstrated the fact by jumping nimbly up and down boxes until I wanted to cry: 'Is there an orthopedic surgeon in the house?' That, it seems to me, is the weakness of the Shakespearean convention; it runs to irrelevant bits of business that merely distract attention from the eternal words.

Admittedly, if he was bored, Yeats could be worse than useless as a critic, and even dangerous. Once he went to see *Cartney and Keaveney*, a popular play of George Shiels, which had been in the repertory for several years, and insisted on its being removed. His reasons might have been those of Dr Johnson; the principal characters in the play glorified idleness and irresponsibility, and this was an improper moral lesson to teach our audience. Long before I joined the theatre we had an argument about Teresa Deevy, whose plays I admired. 'She might have been a good playwright if only she let me reconstruct her plays,' said Yeats, and even for Robinson, who was listening, this was too much. 'A play of Teresa Deevy's reconstructed by you would be rather like a play of Chekhov's reconstructed by Scribe,' he said tartly.

But when Yeats was excited he never missed a point. Once – it was the time after Higgins had already ousted Robinson from first place in Yeats' confidence and esteem – we did a revival of Robinson's early play *The Lost Leader*. It dealt with the idea that Parnell, the greatest of Irish Leaders, had not died, but, suffering from amnesia, had lived on as porter in a small West of Ireland hotel. A hypnotist from London breaks down the old man's secret. It is a good dramatic gimmick, and, as usual with gimmicks, there was a masterly first act, a weak second act and a silly third act – in which Parnell, having delivered a typical Robinsonian appeal to love and good fellowship in Ireland, is killed by a stone thrown by a blind man. Hunt made a beautiful production of it, and the opening of the third act is the only occasion I recall of a décor being applauded in its own right.

The lead was played by an established London actor, and, as usual, Yeats couldn't stand him. We spent the interval together, and Yeats embarrassed me in the foyer by illustrating how he felt the Englishman acted. 'When he should have been calling down the thunderbolt,' he said, reaching towards the ceiling, 'he was picking up matches', and the tall figure bent and groped on the floor. But during the last act Yeats' imagination was working overtime; he had his old affection for Robinson, and nothing could keep him from rewriting the works of people he liked. When I went up to the Boardroom later, Robinson was sitting with his head in his hands while Yeats strode up and down in a frenzy, lecturing him. 'Tell him, O'Connor,' he snorted at me when I entered. 'When Parnell has to tell the mob what to do, he must tell them only what has already happened. There must be no abstractions. Everything must be concrete. He must tell them to do only what the audience knows they themselves have already done.'

'I'm sorry,' Robinson said, looking at the floor. 'I disagree.'

God knows I sympathized with Robinson, being lectured like a schoolboy on his first night, because I had been lectured myself in my time and hadn't liked it, but I knew Yeats was right again. Nothing could have rescued that feeble last act but some such impudent piece of theatrical dexterity.

It was a grave mistake not to take up Yeats on those wild ideas of his, for, apart from anything else, if you couldn't do the job yourself, he was only too pleased to do it for you. He had the ultimate brazenness of the great performer, the man to whom the audience was merely an instrument, and any refusal to use the instrument he regarded as 'barren pride' – the phrase he used when dismissing a friend of mine who had refused to accept any suggestions for the improvement of his play. He was not afraid to accept suggestions himself – 'She might be that stately girl that was trodden by a bird' is supposed to be the suggestion of a poet he particularly disliked – though he did kick up a great pother before accepting them. He hissed with rage when I told him that 'Made Plato's tolerance in vain' was not English, but all the subsequent editions have 'Made the Platonic tolerance vain, and vain the Doric discipline', in spite of the nasty assonance.

In plays that nominally are not his, one can sometimes see his workmanship in the 'properties', the things that are actually on the stage when the play opens – Salvini's 'chair'. In *On Baile's Strand* they are the cooking-pot and the stool. Once he told me how he and Lady Gregory had worked on *The Rising of the Moon* until he was exhausted and sank onto a piano stool. That gave him the idea. 'A barrel!' he cried. 'We must have a barrel!'

Towards the end of his life a young dramatist submitted a bad play on a theme that seemed inspired. A party of pilgrims is setting out from an Irish provincial town on foot to an Italian hill-shrine when the father of one of the girl pilgrims falls ill and she has to stay behind to nurse him. She makes the pilgrimage, walking about the sickroom, but when the pilgrims reach the shrine they find her there before them, kneeling at the altar. Yeats was ill at the time, so I went to his house to talk the play over with him, and as we talked the old man's mask was dropped and I saw the face of the boy behind. It was astonishing to see the reserve of energy he could throw into any literary project: of course the energy was nervous, not physical, and left him exhausted, and one felt guilty at having excited it, but less guilty than when, as sometimes happened, one felt one was boring him. The finest scene he planned took place outside the heroine's house while she made her pilgrimage round the room, unaware of being watched, while the awed villagers interpreted every movement of hers in terms of a real landscape. 'Now she's climbing a hill. It's a steep hill. Now she is stopping and pulling up her skirt. It must be a mountain stream she is crossing.' As he described it, I could even see an Italian landscape emerging.

Though I didn't realize it at the time, it was the only sort of play that made any profound appeal to Yeats. It was a mystery, and all the great early plays of the Abbey Theatre – with the solitary exception of Colum's – were mysteries.

Now I am sorry that after that evening, with a masterpiece 'ready made to my hand', I got cold feet. I had a vague feeling that Yeats and I had been able to construct that scenario easily only because a better dramatist had done so already. He was so convinced of the over-all importance of the fable that he once said to me, 'When you want to write a play, write it on the back of a postcard and send it to me. I'll tell you whether you can produce it or not.' I had the feeling that that particular postcard had already been written and mailed. I lunched with the author and begged her to tell me where she might have read it. She couldn't remember, but thought it might have been in a book of Chinese fairytales she had read when she was a child. This gave me new hope and I read every book of Chinese stories I could lay my hands on without finding it. Indeed, it was only long after I had left the theatre that I found it described in a book of Nora Waln's as one of the masterpieces of the Chinese theatre. The curious orientalism of the whole Abbey Theatre movement was visible that evening when an Anglo-Irishman and a mere Irishman tried to compose the scenario of a great modern Irish play round the theme of a great ancient Chinese play whose existence we didn't know of.

19

By this time, I am afraid, I had been led into spiritual pride, as Catholics like myself called it. I had always known that with economy and hard work the theatre could be made self-supporting, but even then we should have nothing to set against a run of bad luck. In a bad week we could lose a couple of hundred pounds, but in a good one we could rarely make more than twenty-five. All that could be changed if only we had a hundred extra seats, and the only hope of fitting these in was to buy the hardware store next door.

I explained to the Board that if the proprietors of the hardware store knew that instead of their going into bankruptcy, the theatre was proposing to buy them out, they would raise the price beyond anything we could afford to borrow from the bank. Then one evening I went to a Board meeting and saw Higgins with a long face. Robinson had sent the stage carpenter round to the hardware store to enquire the price.

I think it was that evening that I lost my head and stamped out of the Boardroom to the little office where Hunt was nervously waiting his summons and asked him angrily, 'Will you accept a contract as Manager for the next two years?' He blushed and stammered, 'I suppose so, if it's offered to me.' I said, 'Don't worry; it will be', and I returned to the Boardroom and drafted the resolution appointing him. It is one of the few decisions I have never regretted, because for two years he ran that theatre as it had not been run since Lady Gregory's day. Soon we had new plays and money in the bank. Though Yeats gave me the credit, it was mainly Hunt's doing.

One evening, when Yeats was in attendance, the Secretary,

before reading out the bank statement, grinned and said, 'Well, gentlemen, I have some good news for you. For the first time in years the theatre has a credit balance.' The credit balance was only three shillings and sixpence, but it meant we need not worry about letters from the bank, threatening to close us down. The directors applauded, and as we left the meeting Yeats asked me to walk with him. When we were approaching O'Connell bridge, where he was to get his bus, he stopped and made one of his formal little speeches. These, like his reminiscences of people he hadn't met for twenty years, were part of his dramatic stock-in-trade, and had the same childlike quality. I wish I could recall its perfection of phrasing; it had obviously been thought out, because as so often with that strange, romantic man, self-accusation blended with congratulation of someone else. It was something like this.

'There's something I wanted to say to you, O'Connor. You may not have realized that I was watching what you did, because I have had to oppose so many of the things you have done, but all the same, I knew they had to be done. Thirty years ago I should have done them myself, but now I am an old man and have too many emotional associations. Thank you.'

But I had my emotional associations as well as Yeats. I knew that Hunt was the one man who could save the theatre at the time, but I also knew that giving him the opportunity had left Lennox Robinson as jobless and penniless as he had found me in Cork a few years before, and it was too neat an example of the classical peripeteia to cast myself for a part in it. I also remembered that when I came to Dublin Robinson was the first to invite me to his house. After a sleepless night I took him to lunch. It is a task I would not wish on anybody. To speak about his drunkness to an older and more distinguished man is a task for one who in Standish O'Grady's phrase is 'not only brazen-faced, but copper-bottomed', and I am lacking in brass. I asked what I could do to help him and he replied quite simply, 'Get me a job.' That was a tall enough order in itself, for the theatre does not run to jobs in which a man can drink himself to death without doing any harm to the institution. 'And if I can get you a job, will you agree to go to a specialist – the theatre will pay.' 'Yes, yes, anything you like,' he said wearily, 'but I must have work.'

There the man was in all his strength and weakness – he could not fight back. If I had offered him a job as uniformed doorkeeper he would have accepted it – and later shown me off the premises with perfect courtesy. What I did not recognize then, what Yeats never recognized (though I suspect that Lady Gregory had her suspicions), was the immense power behind that inertia, fed as it was by masochism and accepting without complaint rebuke, humiliation and even insult. For even if I had understood it then as I understand it now I should still have lacked the ability of the old society woman to shut it out altogether from my mind.

There was only one thing for me to do. A few days before the scene at the Board meeting I had pressed for the appointment of Shelah Richards as Director of the Abbey School of Acting, so I went straight to her and asked to be released from my offer. 'If you want the job for Lennox Robinson, you're welcome,' she said without hesitation. The theatre is a cut-throat business, and actors are of necessity a thankless lot, but not, it seemed, where Robinson was concerned. I only wished I could attract the same sort of devotion. Unfortunately, within a month or two Robinson was turning up drunk to classes, or not turning up at all, and the School of Acting was in as big a mess as the theatre had been.

Meanwhile the final quarrel in the theatre was being staged between Yeats and Higgins on the one hand and Hunt and myself on the other. 'Why do you support Hunt?' Yeats asked me bluntly one night. For want of anything better to say I replied, 'Because we must have a competent man in the theatre.' Yeats drew himself together like an old grandfather clock preparing to strike, and, as he always did whenever he wanted to say something crushing without being personal, told a story. 'My mad brother' (sometimes it was 'my father' and sometimes 'an old aunt of mine') 'once said to me: "What does an artist have to do with competence?"'

I knew that about the main issue between us – the style of acting which Yeats called the Abbey tradition and Higgins called 'porthery' – Yeats was absolutely right, and I preached the same doctrine to Hunt at every opportunity, but not being a theatre man I felt it was my immediate responsibility to get the theatre on its feet, with a repertory of modern Irish plays and a style of acting that suited them. Yeats wanted a continuation of the Senecan style of acting, common in the universities in Shakespeare's day, in which words were all-important, nobody spoke while moving and nobody moved while someone else was speaking for fear of distracting attention from the words – the opposite of the later English naturalistic convention in which beautiful speeches are chopped up and fitted into bits of stage business – picking up matches, for instance. It is like a duet in which two instruments never play together. But the Senecan style must have been out-of-date even in Shakespeare's day. In one of *The Parnassus Plays* there is a scene in which Shakespeare's friends, Burbage and Kemp, give an audition to some university lads trained in the Senecan tradition, and they describe it as resembling a walk with someone who speaks only when he comes to a stile. The Senecan is a purely rhetorical convention and admirable for poetry; the other, the Shakespearean convention, is purely dramatic, and sometimes plays hell with poetry, even Shakespeare's. And how easily I could have got round Yeats if only I knew then what I know now and could have given him the word 'Senecan' to brood over! He was a man who loved pedigrees, even for his canaries, and would have been so happy, murmuring to visitors, 'Our convention, the Senecan, which preceded the convention of Shakespeare. . . .'

But Hunt had been brought up in the Shakespearean convention, and he couldn't take the Senecan style seriously, so that when he produced the plays of Lady Gregory and Yeats he did have a tendency to squeeze the poetry out of them to make room for dramatic effects. Our biggest disaster was with *Deirdre*, and for this I was largely to blame. I wanted to produce *The Player Queen*, my favourite Yeats play. As Hunt wanted occasionally to work with an English actress, we suggested Jean Forbes-Robertson, who had the fairylike coloratura quality that the imitation queen must have. But Yeats had promised the part to an actress with whom he was friendly at the time. She was inexperienced, and since I had heard no favourable account of her I refused to invite her to Dublin. After that, all Yeats would give us was *Deirdre*. Apart from the fact that we didn't like the play, it was quite unsuitable for Jean Forbes-Robertson. It was like asking the perfect Zerlina to play Isolde. I felt even more unhappy when I took Jean out to lunch and she said gaily, 'Well, I don't understand a word of the part, but I've made up a little story of my own that covers it pretty well.'

So, on the first night I gave up my seats to friends from the country and went to the theatre only to check the takings. They were good and the reception – to judge by the prolonged yells that could be heard in the foyer – was overwhelming. I was in the box office when Yeats came staggering up the stairs from the stalls, clutching his head. 'Terrible! Terrible! Terrible!' was all he could bring out. I was certain he was exaggerating, so next evening I went by myself and sat in the back of the gallery. It was even worse than Yeats and Higgins had led me to believe, because they at least had liked Mícheál MacLiammóir as Naisi and I could see no merit in anybody. I felt that all the actors must have heard Jean Forbes-Robertson's 'little story'. None of them could keep still for two minutes, and the play needed all the Senecan starch. Higgins' 'porthery' simply couldn't exist in that Shakespearean atmosphere. Unfortunately it was a great popular success, and its expensiveness forced us to continue it after MacLiammóir left, so Hunt took on the part himself. It should be enough to say that Hunt was half MacLiammóir's build and with less than half his voice, and that it was no use trying to explain to him how an actor in the Senecan convention can build a tremendous climax merely by using fractions of semitones.

Naturally Yeats was furious, and Higgins stormed against Hunt, without, however, having the faintest idea of how to produce the poetic effects he talked of. Instead, he had invented something called 'Peasant Quality' – which the players turned into 'P.Q.' and used the slogan 'Mind your P.Q.'

And yet neither Yeats nor Higgins could see that the English naturalistic convention, applied to new Irish plays and players, produced an exquisite effect that was neither purely Senecan nor naturalistic, but an extraordinary blend of simplicity and polish – 'beauty like a tightened bow'. With the new plays the result was an entirely new style and an entirely new type of actor – represented by Cyril Cusack – that seemed to suit perfectly the sort of theatre we wanted. I doubt if even Hunt knew the secret of what he was doing, for its presence could be detected only because by Friday – unless the players were closely watched – it began to rub off, the opposite of what usually happens in repertory, where the players gradually begin to settle into their parts.

There was an interval of peace when some of the players left to tour America with Higgins as manager. The tour got off to a disastrous start. Hunt was keeping the theatre open with a second company, and we wanted a fair split, reserving a stiffening of the older players, while letting American critics have a glimpse of the new talent being produced by the Abbey. However, the older players, thinking of Hollywood contracts, resented this and got at our American manager, who cabled his own list of players, which we had to accept.

In America Higgins dropped the company altogether, and all the news we could get of them was from American newspapers, which described furious scenes between rival lawyers. Higgins simply ignored our cables, though after a month or so I got one report from him which was a masterpiece of wild humour, but told me nothing we really wanted to know. Blythe wanted to dismiss Higgins by cable and appoint Arthur Shields in his place, but Yeats simply mocked at the idea. 'What you and Blythe want is a three-pound-a-week clerk,' he snorted. 'You can't buy a genius for three pounds a week.' But we didn't want a genius; we merely wanted someone to keep that wretched touring company out of our hair while Hunt went on with the real business of the theatre, which was producing new plays.

And that was no easy task. For years I had been haunted by the subject of the Invincibles, a little group of Dublin terrorists who assassinated the British Chief Secretary in Ireland, Lord Frederick

Cavendish, in 1882. I drafted a play about them. It was a bad subject for me because it is a peculiarly Dublin tragedy and would have needed an O'Casey to handle it. When Hunt agreed to join me as collaborator, putting real theatrical bones into my dramatized history, it became still more unsuitable, because, though in real life he was a brave and patriotic Englishman, as a man of the theatre he felt bound to identify himself with his subject, and no amount of lecturing would keep him from writing lines like 'Christ, we'll cut the throats of all the dirty English bastards!' It is, as Arnold said, the tragedy of the artist – 'we become what we sing' – and I was watching Hugh Hunt turn into a terrorist under my eyes.

During the production two things happened that I shall never forget. One was Cyril Cusack's performance. Hunt had asked me not to embarrass him by attending rehearsals, for fear I should compromise the cause of terrorism any farther, and I had loyally agreed. He suddenly asked me to attend the last rehearsal but one, and speak to Cusack, who was behaving very badly. So far as I was concerned he was Hunt's discovery – a great actor, and, as Hunt explained to me, 'Not Irish at all, you know; straight Cockney.' Cusack played the part of young Tim Kelly, the choirboy who followed his older friend, Joe Brady, the stonemason, to the gallows. I went to the rehearsal and listened in dismay. I knew Cusack's part was vilely written, but he was deliberately ignoring the most commonplace theatrical effects as though they bored him. Maybe they did. At the same time I realized that it was far too late to interfere because anything I suggested would only throw off the other players, particularly Willie O'Gorman, who, as Joe Brady, was carrying the whole play magnificently on his shoulders.

Next day I went to the dress rehearsal and listened to Cusack again. He hadn't changed an iota of his interpretation; he still seemed to throw away every speech, but after a few minutes I began to feel a physical chill in the theatre. I looked round and saw two of the actresses weeping openly. When actors weep at someone else's performance in a dress rehearsal it has to be pretty good.

Out of that unspeakable part Cusack had created something that wasn't in any line of it, a loneliness so terrifying that it made you wonder how the human mind could sustain it. I had always known what a great writer could do. That day showed me what a great actor could do.

The other thing I remember is Robinson's extraordinary behaviour. As a member of the Board he had read and approved the play. He had done more than that. He had taken me aside and pointed out to me the simple but important mistake I was making. I had written the play almost entirely in brief speeches, as a story-teller writes, and ignored the fact that in the theatre brief speeches – the equivalent of the Greek stichomythia – must be interrupted by long, expository ones, to give the actor and audience breathing space. I was grateful and pleased because I felt that Robinson was treating me like a friend, but there was small hope of that. By the time the play was ready for production, word had reached us through the Dublin underground that the Left Wing groups disapproved because they thought the play exploited and carica-tured terrorism, and they proposed to wreck the theatre. On the first night this looked more than likely because Yeats' old girl friend Maud Gonne came in for the first time and took her place in the stalls. There was no riot that night because Maud apparently decided it might not be understood, and the only protest came from a Nazi visitor who thought the play was directed against Hitler and wrote to the papers to say how shocked he was at this defence of tyrannicide. But while the players were still wondering whether or not they would have to fight, Robinson went to a debate at the rival theatre across the road and denounced Hunt and me bitterly for having dramatized a subject that was bound to cause pain to the relatives of the men who had been hanged by the British fifty years before. On the whole, the relatives of the men who had been hanged didn't seem to be too upset, and when Joe Brady's sister arrived at the theatre – to lend us the suit that her brother died in, for our production – Hunt felt it his duty to receive her as if she were royalty.

But everybody in the theatre realized that Robinson's remarks were a stab in the back and that he was trying to provoke a riot of his own. Hayes immediately tabled a resolution demanding his dismissal from the Board. It would have been plain common sense on my part to support Hayes, but before the meeting Yeats invited me to meet him for tea so that he could explain why he must oppose the resolution 'for personal reasons'. He knew he didn't have to tell me what the personal reasons were. Robinson was his friend whom he had already defended against Lady Gregory, and he had been a good friend to Mrs Yeats when she needed friends, and he was adored by Yeats' children. Yeats knew Robinson was in the wrong and was obviously distressed – a different Yeats altogether from the one who knew he was in the right and was determined on proving it to you. I merely told him that in any matter that concerned his peace of mind he could rely on me, which was perhaps disloyal to Hayes, though I don't think Hayes would have regarded it so.

It was a queer, agonizing evening. It began on the theatre backstairs. Yeats was obviously very ill and could only climb a step or two before pausing for breath. It seemed rude to stand behind him for minutes on end, waiting to see him take the next step. If it had been Russell, I should have taken his arm and lifted him up, but I knew Yeats wouldn't tolerate that from me. I could have run ahead and chattered from the top of the stairs, but I had been trying, without much success, to get the other members of the Board to stand up when he came into the room, and that didn't seem right either. He was doing this on Robinson's account, not mine.

At last we got up and he fell into a chair with Robinson on his left-hand side and Hayes at the foot of the table on my right. Hayes moved his resolution quietly – normally he was the quietest of men. Mr MacNamara had been asked to resign from the Board because he had given in to a hot-headed impulse that everyone understood and sympathized with. Could any member of the Board sympathize with Mr Robinson in an act of calculated treachery, and if so how could they justify their behaviour to a loyal colleague like Mr MacNamara? Hayes had the grand manner, and he could be stinging on an occasion like this. He looked directly at Robinson and asked why – since Mr Robinson was so sympathetic with the relatives of the executed men – he had waited until the previous Sunday to express his sympathy. Robinson sat with downcast eyes and did not reply.

Then Yeats made his speech and I have not forgotten the opening words. It began: 'Every member of this Board realizes that Lennix Robinson is no longer responsible for his actions', and went on to say, 'Robinson will apologize for his behaviour and his apology will be published in the Dublin newspapers.' Robinson sat that out too; his very despondency was his greatest strength. It was a technique I was now beginning to recognize. At times it was almost as though he enjoyed his own humiliation, as, with that strong masochistic element in his character, he may have done. And yet I knew he worshipped Yeats and that it must have been agony for him to endure that humiliating apologia, as it was for Yeats to offer it. We were all glad when it ended. After the meeting Yeats left without speaking to him. He was angry at finding himself in the wrong camp and angrier still at having been forced to humiliate a friend in front of strangers.

There was some truth in what he said about Robinson's not being responsible. Robinson wrote an apology which was merely a repetition of everything he had said about Hunt and myself. When Hayes saw it he grew really angry. 'Send that to Yeats!' he said. 'If he's prepared to stand over that, he and Robinson are in this thing together.' I did what he suggested, and by return came a handsome apology, which may or may not have been published. But even that Yeats had to write for him, as I later learned.

There were other signs of mental deterioration in Robinson. He could no longer afford to keep up his home on Dublin Bay. He embarrassed me and delighted Higgins by producing a completely dotty scheme according to which Bernard Shaw ('He has lots of money') would buy the house, set him up as custodian, and he would provide a residence ('at a trifling cost') for younger writers like ourselves with books to finish, which needed to be finished in the beauty and repose of Killiney. He was drifting into the part of the literary panhandler, the famous figure whom every mediocrity in Dublin could afford to patronize. Yet those who knew him in those years still remember little touches of consideration and sweetness which showed that the old Robinson was still there.

PART FOUR

THE DEATH OF YEATS

20

THE row between Yeats and Higgins and Hunt and me had now got completely out of hand. It isn't, as I have said, that most of the time I was not entirely on Yeats' side and didn't try again and again to explain to Hunt the sort of acting that the older type of play required. There was, for instance, the little matter of *Dervorgilla*, Lady Gregory's beautiful one-act play, which I had insisted on restoring to the repertory. Hunt mistakenly gave the part of Dervorgilla to a young and inexperienced actress, and – again I think mistakenly – allowed the tremendous final speech of the old queen to be broken by the young actress' sobbing (as though Dervorgilla, realizing that because of her love affair with the King of Leinster, Ireland had become a subject province and herself a woman whose memory would be execrated, would regard it merely as another example of the old saying that 'the woman always pays'). This was a clear example of the way English naturalistic production inevitably turns Deirdre into 'The Second Mrs Conchobhar'. I squabbled with Hunt about it at the dress rehearsal, and later, visiting Yeats on other business, told him what I had done. 'Is it ever permissible for an actor to sob before the final curtain?' I asked, and Yeats snapped, 'Never.'

During that visit Yeats was in a state of delight over a Chinese carving in lapis lazuli which some friend had given him, and he was writing his acknowledgment in verse. It was characteristic of him that when he was in a mood of excitement every casual conversation got swept in to the poetry, sometimes with alarming results to the logic. That night my Advice to the Players somehow got itself embodied into Yeats' thank-you poem as:

> Yet they, should the last scene be there,
> The great stage curtain about to drop,
> If worthy their prominent part in the play,
> Do not break up their lines to weep.

Once, when O'Faolain and I were at the house together, Yeats read us the Meru poem on the Trinity and asked if we understood it. O'Faolain, being both clever and well-brought-up, replied, 'Oh, yes', but I said, 'I don't understand a word of it, W.B.' Higgins reported that Yeats had said to him later that night, 'O'Faolain and O'Connor were here, and I read them the Meru poem, and O'Faolain said he understood it and he didn't, and O'Connor said he didn't understand a word of it, and he understood it perfectly.' (Nothing would ever persuade Yeats but that I was cleverer than I was.) And sure enough his next poem in the series begins, 'Although you said you understood no word'.

Still, I don't think he ever understood that I was on his side, or maybe he felt I was but was too arrogant to admit it. Next time he came back to Dublin from the Riviera, he and I had one of our biggest set-tos. By this time I was convinced that it was impossible to keep Hunt on over the opposition of Yeats and Higgins, which was usually unreasonable and often ungenerous.

If I couldn't have Hunt I wanted Denis Johnston, but the very name of Johnston made Higgins cringe. Like most of the other members of the Board, he wanted to keep the theatre under his own personal supervision, and if he couldn't do this with Hunt, what chance had he with Johnston? Like members of the Opposition everywhere, he wanted a weak government, and I finally agreed that we should look round for some young man of the theatre whom Hunt could train. Hunt, who was completely selfless in his devotion to the theatre and in Roman times would probably have trained the lion to devour him piecemeal in order not to spoil the show, chose two young men he thought he could train and give them plays to produce. I went to the rehearsal of one of them and said I was not interested. I didn't go to the other's rehearsals because he had cast himself for the principal part and would have so much trouble producing himself that he would have no time for the other members of the cast.

What sank me completely was Hunt's production of *The Playboy of the Western World*, with Cyril Cusack as Christy Mahon. This was as misconceived as it was magnificent. Cusack – the greatest Irish actor I have seen – interpreted the part brilliantly, but there is nothing in it that the words do not interpret better; as with *Deirdre* and *Dervorgilla* it was the English inability to get out of the way of poetry. The long surging lines, which must be spoken in the manner of Racine's alexandrines, either in one breath or with the trained singer's tricks of imperceptible breathing, were broken up by the elaboration of points that were only a distraction, and were of the same order as picking up matches.

Higgins and I had an angry scene about it. Yeats was abroad; Higgins was in the position of unofficial widow, and I could not get him to admit how sensitive the production was, how lovingly every detail of background and lighting had been re-created, or how beautiful Ann Clery was as Pegeen Mike. All he could see was that Cusack had chopped up the 'porthery', and in Hunt's absence he went to Cusack's dressing-room to make a scene about it. I only learned this when Hunt told me he intended to complain, and I felt he was justified in doing so. There are better ways of indicating to a great actor that you disapprove of his performance than by going to his dressing-room when he is overwrought and starting a fight.

So I supported Hunt and Cusack, while Higgins complained to Yeats, who, after his return, arrived at the next Board meeting looking like the terrible judge of Michelangelo's *Last Judgment*. He ignored me and delivered a long speech on the sanctity of the Abbey tradition and a violent attack on Hunt's *Playboy*. That made me furious to begin with. For a man of the theatre to criticize a performance he hasn't even seen is unforgivable, and I had no intention of letting Yeats get away with it. When my turn came I replied at length and said that, while I agreed with him about the speaking of poetry, I could find no evidence for the existence of a tradition in the theatre except a lot of bad acting. This was trailing my coat with a vengeance, and the reader is fully entitled to blame me. The very memory of this hurts me now, and I often blame myself for this deliberate trampling on Yeats' toes, but at the time I felt that Yeats had trailed his coat a bit, and if he was going to gang up with Higgins and his infernal 'porthery' I was going to gang up with Hunt.

Then Yeats made a serious tactical mistake, which left him wide open. He lost his temper and turned the attack on me. 'And you –' he stammered, 'you said you'd try to find some man to take Hunt's place, and when two young men produced their plays you weren't even there.' This was true enough so far as it went, and I had an answer to it (one of the young men was Cusack, whom I was defending), but at this stage our difference had gone beyond discussion of the Abbey and it was Higgins who had come between us. I had Yeats where I wanted him. 'If you're dissatisfied with my work as a member of this Board, you can have my resignation right now,' I said, 'but while I am a director of this theatre there is one thing I will not do, and that is reply to green-room gossip.'

There was no doubt about who had won that round, because Yeats was the most loyal of colleagues, and he *had* repeated green-room gossip, only the green-room gossip had not originated with the theatre company, but with Higgins, and I hadn't the sense to see it. Yeats went white. It was the sort of imputation he could not bear, and at our last meeting, just before he went to France to die, the charge still rankled, for when he wanted to tell me that he trusted me he had to begin with the complaint that I did not trust him. '*You* think I listen to green-room gossip....'

But if I had won that round, he won the match, because no one but myself would stand up to him in one of his bullying moods. Hunt was debarred from all further productions of Synge, Lady Gregory and Yeats; and, in atonement to Synge's memory, Higgins was invited to produce a 'classical' performance of the *Playboy* directed by one of the old players.

Higgins was a good poet, but he couldn't produce a child's

recitation. He went into a dither of excitement, begging the players to remember their 'Peasant Quality' and pronounce every 'st' as 'sht' and say 'Cashelbar' instead of Castlebar'. This seemed to me exactly the same fault of excessive naturalism that Hunt had been blamed for. The performance was a nightmare. Such an evening of uncontrolled caterwauling and wailing was never heard in any theatre, while the players tried to demonstrate their 'Peasant Quality' and did their best to imitate Higgins' imitation of a County Mayo accent. Hunt's splendid lighting was entirely dispensed with, and instead every stage light was turned on full, masked by yellow screens, which, of course, reduced the apparent depth of a stage that was impracticably shallow anyhow to about six feet. Sitting in the stalls with Yeats, I kept expecting that every time a player rushed on stage he or she was going to land in my lap. There are at least six imperative changes of lighting, all of which were blandly ignored. People came on with a lantern, and the light didn't change; they went off with it and the light didn't change, and finally Pegeen Mike quenched the only conceivable source of illumination, and still the stage remained looking like Times Square on Christmas Eve.

'What do you think of that?' I asked Yeats as the curtain fell.

'Oh, very fine, very fine,' he replied with an abstracted air.

'I think it's absurd,' I said and walked out of the theatre.

But no reasonable human being could fight for long with Yeats. As well as a successor for Hunt I had to find a successor for Tanya Moiseiwitsch, who insisted on leaving with him, and I arranged to send Yeats' daughter, Anne, who had been assisting Tanya, to study stage design with Baty and Jouvet in Paris. I had warned Anne Yeats that Baty was a magnificent director with no notion of acting, and Jouvet a magnificent director of players with no notion of stage design. God alone knows what complicated intrigue Yeats saw in this, for it would simply never have occurred to him that I had been watching his daughter's work with interest, but as no one was allowed to excel Yeats in courtesy he arranged to publish a superb edition of my translation of 'The

Lament for Art O'Leary', with coloured drawings by his brother, Jack.

A short time later I invited myself out to Rathfarnham to present a friend of mine to Mrs Yeats. At once Yeats started explaining to me that as a father he could not possibly allow his daughter to go to Paris unprotected, and that she must go to the Old Vic instead, where she could be looked after by some aunt, cousin or friend. I replied that nothing I had seen in the Old Vic had given me the idea that we had anything to learn from it and that I wouldn't consent to spend a penny of the theatre's money on sending Anne there. Yeats grew sulkier and sulkier, but George, seeing us to the door later in the evening, lifted my spirits by doing a dance step in the hall. 'That old bully!' she said. 'It's about time someone stood up to him. He's always trying to push people around.'

It was not the first time she had saved an evening for me, but it may perhaps explain why I shut Higgins up when he talked of the Yeatses' domestic affairs. I knew the apparent childish selfishness of Yeats, because once when I was seeing him home, he went to his club, and told me that George was ill with some infectious disease and that he couldn't go home. I, thinking of George by herself in the house, said 'Oh, that's awful!' and Yeats replied mournfully, 'Yes. You see, I can't even get at my books.' But I also saw the other side, which apparently Higgins didn't see. Once, when we went in a taxi to some Board meeting, I paid the taxi driver and Yeats grabbed the money frantically from his hand and created a scene while he tried to find money of his own – always a difficult task for him as he never could make out where his pockets were. I said, 'Oh, stop it, W.B.', and he turned on me. 'You don't understand, O'Connor,' he gasped. 'I wouldn't mind, but my wife would never forgive me.' Maybe only a storyteller can understand that, but I knew that a man who worried about what he was going to tell his wife about who paid the taxi fare was a man in love, whatever anybody else might think.

By this time I was in a bad state of unrest myself. I was unwell, and now, to the difficulty of holding down a job as librarian, running a runaway theatre and trying to write, was added an annulment action in the ecclesiastical courts that might go on for years. My publisher, Harold Macmillan, had said to me in his wise way, 'You've reached the stage where you must decide whether you're going to be a good writer or a good public servant. You can't be both.' I knew he was right, but it wasn't an easy choice. The only security I had ever known was the position I had made for myself, and I knew that once I gave it up I should never find another. I had gotten myself too much of the reputation of a firebrand. While I hung on to my job I could be ejected only with difficulty, but once out of it there would be plenty to see that I never got another chance. At last I gathered up what little courage I possessed, threw up my job, and went to live in County Wicklow.

And that, in some ways, was even worse. A writer is as conditioned to his methods of work as any old horse, and I found that the long day's leisure away from the activities that interested me was simply something I was not trained to take advantage of, so that when I did sit down to work at my usual hour after supper the day's idleness had already drained and dispirited me so that I wrote without aim or conviction.

Another source of anxiety was that I knew that until the annulment went through I should be a source of danger to the theatre. This was precisely the sort of weapon that its enemies would use, and not long before, when Hayes and other members of the Board had sat joking about a love affair between two of the players which had caused some scenes, I had said, 'This is no joking matter, and if I hear of it officially I shall ask for the resignation of both. The theatre is more important than anyone's feelings.' I decided to see Yeats and ask him to let me resign quietly. Hayes knew what I intended doing and, in his wise way, he tried to dissuade me. I liked being dissuaded, because there was nothing I wanted to do less than resign, but I had the puritanical sense I had inherited from Mother and Corkery and felt that though what I chose might be wrong I still had to choose. Yeats and I went out to dinner, and I explained how I felt about it. I even explained what I had already said about the players, and he was amused. 'That is quite different, O'Connor. If it had been a question of a Protestant director and a Catholic actress, I should have asked for his resignation immediately. But a Catholic director and a Protestant actress – we are unassailable.' Besides, in his romantic way he was thrilled by the more ceremonial usage of the ecclesiastical courts and said wistfully, 'I suppose the case will go to Rome', obviously thinking of the fine figure he would have cut himself in an atmosphere of Renaissance diplomacy.

And then, growing serious and becoming the Yeats I loved, he said, 'I can't accept your resignation, O'Connor. I know you think I listen to green-room gossip' – the old rebuke that he brooded over for months – 'but when I die I want to leave my theatre to you and Higgins.' There, again, was the essential Yeats – the man who never ignored a rebuke or an obligation.

This opened the way for a general discussion, and I begged him again to bring Denis Johnston in as producer. Of course I was attacking the obsession with Higgins, and the stubborn Yeats was aroused by his loyalty. Because he was feeling fond of me, he let me down lightly. Whenever he wanted to compliment me he quoted his wife as his authority and he said: 'You and George have exactly the same admiration for Denis Johnston. George made me listen to a radio programme of his on the Siege of Derry, and it was a masterpiece. But I can't help thinking he is a young man who would want his own way.' I knew perfectly well that Johnston would want his own way – was there ever a gifted man who didn't? – but I wondered what he thought Higgins and Blythe wanted.

The discussion swayed to and fro as such discussions must between a young man and an old one. Then he said sternly: 'At the next meeting of the Board I attend I want you to propose the dismissal of Robinson. When you quarrelled with him before, I knew you were right, but I had to oppose you; I had certain personal commitments. They no longer exist. I know Robinson is a danger to the theatre, and he must go.'

Well Yeats might talk of commitments. For years I had been

watching what George Yeats was doing for him – and long after his death she told me that I was the first person who recognized that she was doing a job for him. But she wasn't being fair, any more than Yeats or Robinson or I was being fair. How could any of us be fair? I worshipped George Yeats, and I admired Robinson because it seemed to me that he too understood what she was doing. So I said to Yeats, 'Having accepted a public apology from Robinson I can't very well ask for his dismissal.' 'That was because you didn't know who wrote the public apology,' said Yeats. 'I wrote it, and I said to him, "Sign that." And he signed it,' Yeats added bitterly, and I knew that this was what upset him, and that if Robinson had pulled himself together and told Yeats to go to hell, Yeats would have been so proud of him that no one on earth could have attacked him.

While we ate, he went on, reminiscing about their relationship and the dozens of minor treacheries it had involved. And yet more revealing of Yeats' real nature were his last words on Robinson. After he had told me everything he had against him, he raised his finger and said sternly, 'But remember, O'Connor, that was Lennix Robinson the drunken intriguer, not Lennix Robinson who was your friend and mine.' Even today I can hear Yeats' voice as he uttered that magnificent line. I never did think him worth a damn as a love poet, but as a poet of friendship I felt he had no equal. How else could he have written:

> For friendship never ends
> And what if mind seemed changed
> And it seem changed with mind;
> When thoughts rise up unbid
> On generous things that he did,
> And I grow half-contented to be blind?

At times like this Yeats fascinated me. I had seen it once or twice before, most clearly on the night when Miss Horniman's death was announced, and he suddenly poured forth stories of her and her friends which are not in the official histories. It was not so much that the stories were particularly interesting in themselves, but that they threw such an extraordinary light on his own character. Anyone who had listened to him talk of Lennox Robinson in earlier days might have been forgiven for regarding him as a foolish, fond old man; listening to him when he suddenly decided to talk freely one realized that the foolish, fond old man was only half the personality, the personality that made the poetry, but that beneath it was another sort of personality altogether, sensitive and compassionate, but watchful, cool and without illusion, the mind of a novelist rather than that of a poet. This, of course, was what gave him his extraordinary capacity for development, and even in the few years I had known him I had seen his poetry getting nearer and nearer to my own ideal of poetry. He warmed my heart so much that night that I picked up enough courage to pay him a compliment. I said that if God gave him another ten years he would be the greatest lyric poet who had ever lived. He took this modestly, as Mother took praise of her good looks, and said, 'All the things I wanted to do when I was eighteen I am doing now that I'm an old man.' He was, and with the craziest of equipment. He was writing popular songs with no one but Higgins to give him a hand with the tunes, and poetry that has much of the quality of Old Irish verse on the basis of some translations of mine.

But if he thought that Higgins and I were going to perpetuate the sort of theatre he had dreamed of when he was young, he was very wide of the mark. All the same, things looked promising. Suddenly the government offered a vast sum of money for the rebuilding of the Abbey as a national theatre. Yeats was enthusiastic. It looked as though after his death the theatre would be continued as an institution like the Comédie Française; he had heard me say at Russell's graveside that we had grown up in a country without institutions, and he would have wished the theatre to be one of them. Everybody was enthusiastic but myself. When Blythe produced his draft agreement with the government I had to point out that all we were doing was handing over everything we possessed to the government with no guarantee that we should have the least voice in the eventual policy of the theatre. I was then asked to draft an agreement of my own, and I did, and took it to Yeats for his approval. We went through it clause by clause. He was in an emotional state and talked of what it meant to him that, after all the hostility and violence, he, Synge and Lady Gregory should at last be accepted by their own people. I felt just the same; and I think the proposal of mine that pleased him best was that the main theatre must be called the Gregory Theatre. But the money made me unhappy and in the middle of our conversation I dropped my usual brick.

'Hasn't it occurred to you that we have created vested interests?' I asked, and Yeats gave me an angry look and said bitterly, 'Did you think I wasn't aware of it?'

Nowadays I wonder if he wasn't, and if that cool, watchful intelligence had not already warned him of what was going to happen after his death. Nothing had warned me except an old fear of money in the arts, and yet God knows that I should have been made suspicious by the peculiar things that were happening about me. I had just been involved in a most peculiar row about Yeats' play *The Herne's Egg*. I should have had more sense, but at the time the incident completely befuddled me. Yeats had read it to me while he was writing it, and, apart from one of our usual wrangles about a music-hall joke in the first scene, I had admired it greatly. But when it was submitted to the Board at a meeting not attended by Yeats, the members rejected it because it was obscene. Only Ernest Blythe supported me, and he did so on the grounds that the play was so obscure that no one would notice that it was obscene. This was not what I felt at all, and it seemed to me intolerable that the Board which Yeats had selected himself should coolly reject one of the finest plays of its founder. Hayes became really violent and threatened to resign if it was produced. When I argued with Hayes afterwards, he told me that Higgins had assured him that Yeats' intention was that the seven men who rape the priestess should represent the seven sacraments. This interpretation appeared to me to be the utmost nonsense, but I saw no reason to disbelieve Higgins' story – did I say I was simple-minded? – for I knew that when Yeats was bored or depressed he was capable of saying the most outrageous things. (Indeed, I had heard him not long before tell a young woman who had drunk up his entire ration of whiskey for the night that 'the Blessed Trinity was an invention of a homosexual monk'.) But I did know Catholic doctrine as Higgins – and Hayes apparently – didn't, and I could not see how anybody of reasonable intelligence could accept such a stupid interpretation. Now, the play isn't very difficult. Any reader of Yeats can test that argument for himself. Clearly, the seven men represent the sciences and the priestess revealed religion, while the rape is merely a stylization of the nineteenth-century assault on religion. From the point of view of Christian orthodoxy you could comfortably produce *The Herne's Egg* in any ecclesiastical seminary. Indeed, an ecclesiastical seminary might be about the only place you could produce it where it would be fully understood. But I could not persuade Hayes, a really pious man – and by pious I don't mean prissy – that Yeats had no intention of being blasphemous.

Finally, in a fit of exasperation, I said I would produce the play myself at my own expense. When I told Yeats, he turned on me with real anger, and I saw that under all the good-humoured detachment he was bitterly hurt at the rejection of his beautiful play by a group of nonentities. 'And why did you not insist on its being produced when you had a majority of the Board behind you?' he shouted. I didn't know what to say, because the meeting had taken place some time before, and I could not immediately recall the details. I fobbed him off with Hayes' threat of resignation and said we'd had too many resignations. It wasn't until later that I remembered that nobody but Blythe had supported me, and that Higgins, Yeats' friend, was not only one of the play's bitterest opponents at the meeting, but was the person who had influenced Hayes by relating what Yeats was supposed to have said. All Yeats' information came from Higgins, and I was the one who had been presented as having got cold feet. But I still thought the whole thing was a misunderstanding and wondered only if Yeats' supposed blasphemies had not been a misunderstanding as well. I knew it was no use attacking his hero, Higgins, but I did ask him if he had interpreted the play in this way to anyone at any time. He looked at me in bewilderment and grew furious. 'How could I have said anything so silly?' he asked, which was exactly what I had wondered myself. I should have had sense enough to appeal directly to him at the beginning. He was quite right in his joke about me that I didn't think the vast majority of people meant much harm to each other for the greater part of the time, but, all the same, he wasn't too bright himself. Here were we, two grown men being put at cross purposes by schoolboy gossip and intrigue, and neither of us could see through it.

If I had the talent of a comic novelist I should love to describe how that brilliant and delightful man put us all by the ears. Higgins didn't even make a secret of it. He lived in what seemed to be an almost enchanted world of extemporization, imagination and intrigue. After his death, his old friends were approached for the manuscript of his last masterpiece, a play in which the characters were the picture-cards in a pack. I knew that play better than I knew most of my own work. We had listened to it scene by scene and only waited to vote for its production; but, as each of us passed the buck, it became plain that that brilliant play never existed except in Higgins' head.

Yet Higgins was the man he had appointed director of his publishing firm and Managing Director of the Theatre. I had been Managing Director during the absence of the touring company and had asked Yeats how I should conduct myself. 'I asked Lady Gregory exactly the same thing when I became Managing Director,' he said, 'and she told me, "Give very few orders but see that they are obeyed." ' (Knowing her Yeats, the old lady knew that he wouldn't recognize her advice as a quotation from *Don Quixote*.) Nominally Higgins' appointment was for six months, to give us time to find a successor to Hunt. I knew perfectly well that there was no work for a full-time Managing Director, but Higgins entertained himself by doing Hunt's job as well. 'Giving very few orders' was not much in the line of that excitable man. 'My heavens,' he wrote to me, 'things are terrible here – all in a state of chassis. The BBC treated (threatened) to cancel broadcast because we could (couldn't) give the cast Hunt offered – of which we knew nothing. However, had a visit from a BBC official and together we hammered out a suitable cast. Also Hunt never consulted Belfast Opera House *re* our plays for Belfast etc.' (It is only fair to say that Higgins was ill. He had had an attack of Bell's Palsy, which had blasted his handsome face and interfered with his speech, but left him as excitable and enthusiastic as ever.) I admit that the six months' appointment never took me in, for I knew that an Irishman approaches a job in the spirit of the marriage service – 'till death do us part'. But even I never guessed that not only had Higgins dug himself in for life, but that his successor would do the same, and that twenty years later the non-existent job would still be flourishing. 'Vested interests' indeed!

I saw the theatre only at Board meetings, and I did not like the way things were going, with Hunt on the point of departure, and a new man, an Irish-speaking protégé of Blythe, taking over. But everything seemed to move with extraordinary rapidity towards one point – the death of Yeats. A day or two before he left for the south of France for the last time, he had a furious quarrel with Higgins. 'W.B. has left in a difficult temper owing to a personal awkwardness,' Higgins wrote to me. 'Personal awkwardness' was a mild description of Yeats' discovery that Higgins had been playing fast and loose with him all over the shop. After this, Higgins refused to reply to his letters at all, and Yeats, knowing he had only a short time to live, dictated a letter to me. He asked that, if I agreed with him, I should telegraph him and he would take a plane home, dismiss the whole Board of directors, and start again with one chosen by ourselves. But I had no way of knowing how ill he really was, or whether his letter meant anything more than a fit of pique with Higgins, so I wrote him a soothing reply to tell him not to worry. I was in Chester at the time, and as I took my letter to the post I bought a *Daily Telegraph* and read of his death. (Years later, when two young writers had staged a public protest in the Abbey Theatre against its commercialism, I took a book from my shelves and out dropped my last letter to Yeats, unposted, stamped and sealed. I read it between tears, because it brought him back to me so vividly, and shame, to think I could have been such a fool.)

That night I walked for a long time about the old walls of the city, saying over and over the lines from *The Herne's Egg* that seem to me so much a better epitaph than the one he composed for himself. 'Cast a cold eye / On life, on death' is a caricature of Yeats, who was never cold; often angry, often stupid beyond belief, but always young in heart, passionate, involved:

> Strong sinew and soft flesh
> Are foliage round the shaft
> Before the arrowsmith
> Has stripped it, and I pray
> That I, all foliage gone,
> May shoot into my joy.

21

I HAD no idea that night what the death of Yeats would mean to me. In the long run it meant that I took a major decision, one which I have never regretted since, but my blindness at the time, both towards myself and the happenings at the Abbey, guaranteed that I would take the most painful road in changing the course of my life.

I thought that night that I knew what I had lost in Yeats. Not a friend, but somebody who might have been a friend. During his last stay in Ireland his sister, Elizabeth, had asked me straight out, 'Why don't you go and see W.B.?' She was a woman of great beauty, who had what in America would be recognized as the gift of calculated indiscretion – the sort of thing one associates with old American families. And as always when one has to deal with calculated indiscretion I dropped into uncalculated indiscretion and said, 'Oh, I'd be afraid of boring him.' 'I don't think so, you know,' she said innocently, 'because when you do call, he always talks about it. He's very lonely, you know.'

God help us, I did know it. I had known it from the moment George Yeats had sat down beside me at Gogarty's party years before. I went to see Yeats and found him very depressed. He needed a holiday, he said, and I, greatly daring, asked, 'Why don't you come and stay with us? We could look after you very well.' For a moment he didn't know what to say, and then he gave me a boyish grin. 'Old people stay with old friends,' he replied. 'They can be very trying to anybody else.'

When a great man dies, not only does a legend spring up, but a phase of reality ends. Yeats himself realized it when he called one of his own autobiographical books *Ireland after Parnell*. Some day someone will write a book called *Ireland after Yeats*. The things that happen after the death of a man like that have already been happening before he dies, but because he is alive they seem of no great importance. Death suddenly reveals their importance by isolating them.

For a year before his death little things had been happening which had depressed and irritated me. One evening I attended a Board meeting at which the three other directors explained to me with chuckles that I need not read a play by a Minister's wife because it would have to be accepted if we were to keep the government grant. I didn't know which angered me most, the insult to me, the insult to the Minister and his wife, or the insult to our audience, who relied on us to be incorruptible. On another occasion the theatre was running a competition for plays in Gaelic which Blythe was supervising and Mícheál MacLiammóir adjudicating. I learned by the merest accident that Sean O'Faolain had submitted a play. When I enquired what it was like, Blythe said, 'Well, reelly, it wasn't good enough to submit to the adjudicator', and this surprised me, because I did not think there was that much talent among writers in Irish. In the play which was shown to the judge and did win the prize, the principal characters were the Devil and the Blessed Virgin.

Living in the country at Woodenbridge and involved in my own difficulties, it was impossible to be watchful enough. Higgins asked me not to bother reading Cecil Salkeld's play about Germany, *A Gay Goodnight*. 'A ridiculous play; the usual Anglo-Irish rubbish' was how he described it. At the time I didn't know that Higgins and Salkeld had quarrelled and that Salkeld was supposed to have hit Higgins in the theatre bar (somebody was always hitting Higgins). It wasn't until years later, when I saw 'the usual Anglo-Irish rubbish' produced in a stable by a group of amateurs that I realized Salkeld's play was a little masterpiece.

With Yeats permanently gone, I began now to realize that mediocrity was in control, and against mediocrity there is no challenge or appeal. Talent, like any other form of creative activity, has its own dialectic, and from its noisy and bitter conflicts some synthesis emerges, but mediocrity, having neither thesis nor antithesis, leads only a sort of biological life.

But there was worse to come. One evening, after a Board meeting, Higgins asked me in a whisper to remain behind when the others had gone. He was in his usual state of conspiratorial exaltation, and I assumed he had unearthed another plot. He had. When we were by ourselves he opened the minute book and pointed to a resolution that had been proposed by Hayes and passed. At this time I was editing a re-issue of Yeats' old theatre magazine, the *Arrow*; the resolution required me to submit everything I wrote in it to Lennox Robinson for his approval. A short time before, Hayes himself had moved the resolution demanding the dismissal of Robinson from the Board, and Yeats had replied, 'Everybody on this Board realizes that Lennox Robinson is no longer responsible for his actions.' He was now being made responsible for mine, and, being Robinson, probably saw nothing in the least inappropriate about it. Suddenly the door of the Boardroom opened and Hayes was standing there. 'I'm waiting to walk home with you, Michael,' he said plaintively. I could barely speak and said without looking at him that I had some work to do. By this time he realized what Higgins had shown me. 'Oh, very well,' he said in a hurt voice and left. 'And now let me tell you something else,' Higgins said triumphantly. 'You asked why the Board did not give Tanya Moiseiwitsch a dinner before she left. We did, but Blythe insisted that you should not be asked. Here's the report of the dinner, if you don't believe me.'

I left the theatre in a frenzy. I felt that as a result of the death of Yeats I was left alone with a group of men not one of whom I should trust. Hayes' treachery was the thing that mattered most to me because for years he had been my closest friend. A critic of the theatre has described him as an arch-intriguer, though I did not find him so, and his machinations struck me as those of a very innocent and disinterested man. I think that, like many of his generation, he had adopted an idealistic pose too lofty for his own simple character, and that something – something perhaps in me that he couldn't understand – had caused it to break down. Years later, when Higgins was already dead, I was standing at the desk in the National Library when I suddenly felt an arm about my shoulders and heard Hayes say, 'My dear Michael, won't you shake hands with me?' It was one of the few occasions in my life when I shrank away from a man. Remembering the years of good fellowship and kindness, it is something I try to regret, but with little success, for it was more than Hayes I was turning my back on.

What I did regret in 1939 was leaving the theatre of Yeats, and Synge and Lady Gregory, and the end of their dream of a national theatre that would perpetuate their work. The alternative for me was to remain on and fight the Board, not on the terms of the founders, but on the terms of the current members. But there would be no Yeats to whom the members would ultimately have to defend themselves. Genius is often a light by which we occasionally see ourselves and so refrain from some commonness of thought or action that the time allows. I knew then, as I know now, that this kind of in-fighting and intrigue was something I could not carry on alone. Their terms were those of the Nationalist-Catholic establishment – Christmas pantomimes in Gaelic guying the ancient sagas that Yeats had restored, and enlivened with Blythe's Gaelic versions of popular songs and vulgar farces. One by one they lost their great actors and replaced them with Irish speakers; one by one, as the members of the Board died or resigned, they replaced these with civil servants and lesser party politicians.

A great man is one who acts and speaks from a vision of himself. It is not that he is always right and everyone else wrong – often it is the other way round – but that even when he is wrong he is speaking from 'the foul rag-and-bone shop of the heart', the central volcano from which all creation comes. In so far as he interprets his country, as Yeats interpreted Ireland, he has no other source of authority. Once when we were arguing about politics, Yeats quoted a remark of de Valera's of which his enemies were making great capital – 'When I want to know what Ireland thinks, I look into my own heart.' 'Where else could he look?' growled Yeats.

But it takes a large heart to hold even a small country, and since Yeats' death there has been no other that could hold us, with all our follies and heroism.

Years before, he had asked me suddenly one night, 'O'Connor, do you believe you can transmit genius?' I was taken by surprise and did not realize until later that it was his own children he had been worrying about, so I replied, 'Genius? Hardly genius! Talent one can certainly transmit. The Bachs are a good example.' Then I realized that in my usual manner I had said something to make him cross, and he sulked at me for a few minutes. Finally he snorted, 'An old aunt of mine used to say' – the standard beginning for a crushing retort – 'you can transmit anything you like provided you take care not to marry the girl next door.'

It was in war-time England some time later that I came to realize the full significance for me of Yeats' death and my resignation from the Abbey. I was staying with Leonard and Sylvia Strong and had a dream one night which a psychiatrist friend of theirs sought to interpret for me. Suddenly I knew perfectly well what the dream meant and that it was a warning never again to allow the man of action in me to get on top. There was more wisdom in Harold Macmillan's advice than I had thought. Before Yeats died he told me that the time had come to decide whether I wanted to be a good writer or a good public official, and I had resigned my job as librarian. Now I saw that the man of action was still on top: with nothing like Yeats' talent I had been playing Yeats' game. At once I resigned from every organization I belonged to and sat down, at last, to write.